shattered

True Stories of Transformed Lives in Ontario, Oregon

Published in Beaverton, Oregon, by Good Catch Publishing.
www.goodcatchpublishing.com
V1.1

Table of Contents

dedication

This book is for all who have experienced a life-shattering event. To those who feel that they can no longer live a life controlled by addictions, regrets and past mistakes. May you find hope and transformation in the stories of this book.

acknowledgements

I would like to thank Doug Hezeltine for his vision for this book and Kari Massoth for her hard work in making it a reality. And to the people of CLF, thank you for your boldness and vulnerability in sharing your personal stories.

This book would not have been published without the amazing efforts of our Project Manager and Editor, Hayley Pandolph. Her untiring resolve pushed this project forward and turned it into a stunning victory. Thank you for your great fortitude and diligence. Deep thanks to our incredible Editor in Chief, Michelle Cuthrell, and Executive Editor, Jen Genovesi, for all the amazing work they do. I would also like to thank our invaluable Proofreader, Melody Davis, for the focus and energy she has put into perfecting our words.

Lastly, I want to extend our gratitude to the creative and very talented Jenny Randle, who designed the beautiful cover for *Shattered: True Stories of Transformed Lives in Ontario, Oregon.*

Daren Lindley
President and CEO
Good Catch Publishing

introduction

Have you experienced life-shattering events? Do you find yourself asking if the pieces can ever be put back together? What does it look like to be fully restored?

In this book, you will read stories from real people here in the Treasure Valley. Their stories prove that they stopped living in defeat, depression and brokenness. They are fully restored and fully alive!

You may think, "These stories will have nothing in common with my walk in life." With topics like addiction, divorce, suicide, anger and abuse, this book is sure to relate to something you or someone you love is going through. No matter what has brought you to open this book, I only ask that you give it a try.

You can expect riveting stories about how ordinary people have broken free from their past and become extraordinary men and women. I deeply hope that these stories help you push through your tough times and INSPIRE you to push out of the grips of death and pull you into a life restored!

beauty for ashes
The Story of Joseph
Written by Douglas Abbott

It looked disturbingly peculiar, and it was. The fire burned right on top of the snow. The diesel fuel we'd poured on the spot easily overcame the retardant effect of the hard-packed crust of ice, and the flames danced eerily against the white backdrop of the snow-covered hills.

Burning the crimson blotch in front of Uncle Jack's truck had seemed to be the best way to wipe away the awful evidence of what had happened here. Next, we would drive the truck back to the farm and see the room where police had found Uncle Jack's wife and stepdaughter, both shot, carefully wrapped in sheets and placed on the bed. Now the only remainder was bullet holes and bloodstains.

I couldn't stop thinking about the fact that Uncle Jack had been expecting me to come see him just last night. If I had only showed up when I was expected, maybe …

I shook my head violently. It was no use thinking about all that. If I hadn't been so angry, I would have wept. I loved my Uncle Jack. He was so kind to me, inviting me to come live with him when I was a boy. We built his barn together. I couldn't imagine what made him do this.

Even if I dismissed thoughts of my own culpability, I was still left with the fact that the last message I'd conveyed to him was that he and his family weren't important enough for me to show up when I'd told them I would.

Not for the first time, I felt restless in my own skin, living inside it with a person I held in low regard. What Uncle Jack had done somehow underscored this. What else could explain why violent events seemed to follow me? Was it some curse? What would happen next? The disquieting question reverberated in my head while I stood, stunned, watching the fire burn.

ভভভ

My earliest memories are of taking care of my mother, who was diabetic and seemed unable to adjust to her condition. That left me with the responsibility of getting help whenever she lapsed into diabetic shock. This happened each time she took her insulin and then neglected to eat, causing her blood sugar to plummet.

One night I awoke in the wee hours and found Mom slumped motionless in a chair in the living room, a rope of saliva descending from her open mouth. She looked as if she might be dead. Her eyes were like black holes.

I raced out the door in my pajamas. My grandmother lived 70 yards away in an apartment in the rear of her general store. The air was bitterly cold, licking up around my pant cuffs and down the collar of my pajama top. A crescent moon cast a thin sheet of light over the snow-covered ground. I ran as fast as I could go. My bare feet punched through the crust on top of the snow as I went, the ice cutting into my ankles.

I arrived at my grandmother's store and began pounding on the front windows and screaming for help. A few seconds later, I saw a light come on in the back and heard the lumber in the old building shift as my grandmother and Uncle Chad made their way out to me. Soon we were standing in my living room, where Uncle Chad held my mom up in a sitting position so I could pour sugar water into her mouth.

No matter how many times this scene repeated itself, I was always afraid my mom would slide forever into unconsciousness. No one had ever sat down and explained to me what diabetic shock was or that it was rarely fatal. Some of these episodes actually sent her to the hospital, and I wondered when one of these occasions might turn out to be a one-way trip. Finally, when I was older, I became strong enough to hold Mom up without help and pour orange juice or sugar water into her mouth to revive her.

We had a large extended family. Our Thanksgiving and Christmas celebrations were warm and festive. When family members trickled in for the holidays, my world grew immeasurably, filled suddenly with aunts, uncles and cousins. Having playmates was an unusual pleasure. However, the happiness I felt during these family gatherings would evaporate in January as soon as everyone was gone again. There was always a letdown. Guilt began to attach itself to all my joyful experiences.

shattered

I grew up in a bubble, though I didn't realize it at the time. While I was still an infant, my father took my brother and moved away. I wouldn't see either of them again for many years. My mother was completely deaf, and the two of us lived and moved in a fog of silence. I didn't learn to talk until years after I had mastered signing. My grandmother had to force me to talk verbally rather than signing, so deeply had I been drawn into my mother's mute world.

My mother was melancholy and withdrawn. Our communication was limited to whatever task was at hand. When I signed, I was usually acting as an interpreter to help others talk to my mother. I was her mouthpiece to the world. To this day, I cannot recall talking to her about anything substantive.

It was my grandmother who kept me mentally and emotionally alive during those desolate years. The love she lavished on me served as a strong counterweight to my mother's stone countenance. Grandma was strong as an ox, a matriarch who had buried four children but always managed to bring joy to those around her in spite of her pain. Her house was a sanctuary where I felt safe and loved, where none of the bad things could penetrate. Even her sheets had an almost sacred smell.

"God isn't asleep, Joseph. He'll never stop watching over you and protecting you," Grandma told me. "You've gone through some hard things, but God has allowed them for your good. You'll see that one day. The best thing you can do is trust him."

beauty for ashes

I didn't understand principles of faith and trust. I couldn't remember a time when I had ever really rested. I always had the unofficial responsibility of standing vigil for Mom. I thought if I relaxed for a second, her diabetes would overtake her. This same sense of perpetual responsibility became my default setting. I came to believe that my watchfulness was the only thing standing in the way of a thousand unspecified disasters. I moved through life like a clenched fist.

While I was still in elementary school, Grandma sold her store, and Mom moved us to Parma, Idaho, a hamlet about 16 miles away from Grandma. It might as well have been a hundred. We had no car, and I had nothing but a well-used bicycle with slow leaks in the tires.

Our dislocation darkened my world considerably. The sanctuary of Grandma's fragrant house, the comforting presence of my aunts, uncles and cousins, the proximity of the farms — all of it had been whisked out of my life as though it had never existed.

I suffered through weeks of moping and crying spells. There was nothing pleasant or uplifting in my life anymore, nothing but the daily severity of my mother's impoverished world. Worst of all, I no longer had Grandma to turn to for help whenever Mom's diabetic incidents occurred. She had been to the hospital in the past because of her illness. Now there was no one to take us there when the next occasion should arrive.

However, the heaviest burden of all was yet to come. My mother's despondent moods had become more and more pronounced, and she shared her dark thoughts freely with me. In times when she was particularly miserable, it was increasingly common for her to tell me, "I'm going to kill myself," her hands slashing out the dreadful statement.

I knew Mom well and had seen proof enough of the deepening crevasse inside of her. I had no doubt that her intention to commit suicide was sincere, so I took to hiding our knives, scissors and anything else I thought she might employ to end her life. It became a strange, unhappy sort of game. She would make suicidal gestures, and I would hide everything that could be used as a weapon. Then, a day or two later, she would be cooking and ask me what had happened to the knives. I would produce them for her, only to hide them again the moment her dark speech resumed.

While these things were going on, I was barely 9 years old. My experience with the public school system was unmemorable. With regard to Mom's descent into darkness, I had a limited arsenal to work with. I had no idea how to help her in any meaningful way. It never occurred to me to talk to an adult about what was occurring under our roof. I had the strong sense that to do this would be an unforgivable violation of my family's privacy, particularly since our neighbors were essentially strangers now. I didn't realize that if Mom should suddenly be out of the picture, I would probably end up living with Grandma or on one of the family farms. I believed Mom's death would mean utter ruin for me, all the more because, in my mind, it would essentially be my fault.

Sometimes the darkest moments in life come out of the blue. This had seldom been truer than it was at the end of a long, spectacularly sunny day I spent with a new friend named Kent a few months after we moved to Parma. We had done it all that day, including catching frogs and snakes and jumping the creek with our bicycles. Kent had even helped me finish assembling a new model truck my mom had given me that morning. I had scratched my head in perplexity when she gave it to me, since items like this were never in our budget. I still don't know if her unusual gesture had anything to do with the events that followed.

After Kent and I had worn ourselves out on the creek and about the town, we parted ways for the day. I stopped at a local café and asked the waitress, Julie, if I could leave my model truck there with her. She took it and placed it behind the counter for safekeeping. I climbed back on my bicycle and headed for home.

I arrived at the house to find a strange man sitting with Mom in our living room. Strictly speaking, he wasn't a stranger; I knew he was the father of one of my local acquaintances. However, I hadn't had so much a conversation with him. Nor, to my knowledge, had Mom. And I couldn't remember a single occasion when I had come home to find a man visiting with Mom — not even one who was familiar.

The air in the place was heavy. I knew something was

wrong. Mom was acting strange, both physically and in her mannerisms. Although I had never seen it before and hence couldn't put my finger on it, her blood sugar had spiked, causing her to behave oddly. Every other time she'd had a diabetic issue it had been *low* blood sugar, not *high*. I didn't recognize the lethargic symptoms she was displaying. In addition to this, something involving this man had thrown the atmosphere of the house out of kilter.

"Hey, sport," the man greeted me when I came into the living room. He offered me a clammy handshake and grinned at me mirthlessly. There was something stiff in his manner that overshadowed the friendly front he was projecting. "Hey, my son's down at the river. Why don't you ride down there and join him? He's fishin' up a storm!"

Even if this man's demeanor hadn't been so strange, the fact was that dusk was falling rapidly. It made absolutely no sense to be contemplating a trip to the river at this hour.

"C'mon now! Time's a wastin'!"

Everything in me was telling me to stay. However, I was a passive boy, and the man was insistent. "Go on down there, I say! I'm tellin' you, m'boy's pulling catfish out of the river right now. Go on!"

I kept looking at Mom for guidance, but she was scarcely engaged in the conversation.

I tried to compromise. "Well, I'll just go down to the café and get my truck. I'll be back in a little bit." I looked at Mom once more, but she just gazed at the floor.

beauty for ashes

The café was only three blocks away, so it didn't take me long to get back to the house. While I was still crossing the porch, I realized why the man had been so insistent about my leaving. The front door was shut in spite of the summer heat. I could hear their voices coming from the living room, husky with passion. I walked into the living room and found the man entwined with my mother on the sofa. I didn't fully understand what was taking place, but I knew something was very wrong.

My mother looked up at me with surprise in her face. She signed abruptly, "Get out. Leave."

The day we had moved here, Grandma had put a list of phone numbers next to the phone on the wall in the kitchen. Her number was on it, as well as those of all my aunts and uncles in Treasure Valley.

I pulled the sheet of paper off the wall as I was headed out the door. I had a single dollar in my wallet, which Grandma had given me the same day she'd tacked the numbers to the wall.

"Keep this in your wallet," she told me, holding the bill out with one hand while the other was on my shoulder. "Don't spend it. Use it in case of an emergency." I had never thought about the meaning of the word "emergency," but I felt sure that this present situation qualified.

I pedaled back down to the café and asked Julie to give me change for the dollar. I stuffed the 10 dimes into my pocket and rode back toward the house, where there was a phone booth on the corner. I unfolded the list of numbers, put a dime in the phone and dialed Uncle Wade, who owned a dairy farm about 30 minutes away.

"Uncle Wade, there's a strange man at the house with my mom. I'm *afraid*."

I couldn't articulate the situation for my uncle, but my tone of voice was enough.

"Okay, just hang tight. I'm on my way."

It was nearly dark as I crawled up under the low boughs of an evergreen tree that sat between the house and the road. I settled in and waited for my aunt and uncle to arrive.

About 20 minutes later, while I watched through a screen of evergreen needles, the man emerged on the path that led from the back of the building (where our unit was), got in his truck and left. I climbed out from under the evergreen and returned to the house.

Mom was angry when I told her I had called Uncle Wade.

"You had no right to call him!" she signed, her hands flying furiously. "I can have company here if I like. You shouldn't have done that."

Uncle Wade arrived and scolded Mom for being indiscreet, no doubt guessing what kind of business the man had been there on. However, there was little to say now that her visitor was already gone. Uncle Wade left again after a few minutes. However, as I pieced together later, he and Aunt Patty didn't leave straightaway. Working from the assumption that Mom was planning to punish me, he got in his truck and drove around the block.

beauty for ashes

Meanwhile, I was left standing with Mom in the kitchen. Dusk had fallen. I stood across from her trying to read her features in the dim light coming from the hall. She looked back at me with an expression I had never seen on her face before. There were palpable waves of bitterness coming off her. I felt them as though they were gusts of wind.

"I'm going to kill myself," she told me. The moment her hands had signed the words, she reached into the dish drainer, grasped the hickory handle of a butcher knife and plunged it into her stomach. Before I could react, she crumpled to the floor. I was frozen as I looked down at my poor mother's body, folded in half, her face contorted with pain. A crimson pool began to form underneath her. I heard a high-pitched wailing that increased in volume, filling the entire house. As I reached up to cover my ears, I realized the sound was me, screaming at the top of my lungs.

The next thing I was aware of was Uncle Wade, who had returned and was standing next to me in the kitchen looking down at Mom.

"What do you think you're doing, Arlene!" he scolded, evidently forgetting her deafness. He reached down and grasped her arm, apparently intending to haul her to her feet.

"She stabbed herself!" I screamed at him. Then he saw the blood, gathered her up and laid her on the couch in the living room. He took a towel and put pressure on the wound, while Aunt Patty dialed the phone for help. I remember looking at her as she dialed, her hands trembling. Our eyes met, and I told her, "I'm afraid."

She looked back and said softly, "Me, too."

The EMTs huddled over my mother in the small living room for what seemed like ages. I wanted to scream at them to *hurry up*. They seemed to be moving much too slowly. Finally, after they had done their work, they gathered up the stretcher, slid her into the back of the ambulance and sped to the hospital.

My recollection of the events that followed is a patchwork. I remember standing outside my mother's hospital room looking in at her through the thick glass. She was motionless, and I assumed she was still alive. She might have looked peaceful if not for all the tubes and wires connecting her to the medical instruments.

It wasn't long before the rest of the family had arrived at the hospital behind us. The next thing I remember was hearing Aunt Katrina wailing in the hallway outside my mother's room. I knew Mom was dead, but I did not cry. In the bizarre frame of mind I was in during that time, I found it somehow odd that everyone was so upset. Through some strange internal mechanism, my emotions had been muted.

At Mom's graveside service, several of my aunts and uncles urged me to be strong for Grandma. "She's lost five of her children," some of them told me. I was too young to fully appreciate a 70-year-old woman being preceded in death by five of her children in this age of medical triumphs and extended life expectancy. What I understood perfectly was the part about being strong, which I took to mean that I must not cry.

Accordingly, I shed no tears as we stood in a clumsy circle around the casket, all dressed in dark colors that contrasted strangely with the bright sun. In the faces around me were grief and bewilderment. None of us could explain why we were here. My mother was only 37.

I remember nothing of what the clergyman said, only that his voice was somber as he preached and read to us from his battered Bible. When the time came to pay our respects, one of my uncles nudged me from behind, and I moved toward the open casket. My mother lay inside, looking so peaceful that she might have been asleep. I wanted to touch her, but I thought I would be breaching some protocol. None of the others touched her, either. For years afterward, I wished I could have another chance to put my hand on her cheek as I said goodbye.

In the aftermath of Mom's death, Grandma took me into her home. Even as I obtained much-needed rest there, I was tormented by guilt. I had been Mom's primary caretaker for as long as I could remember. I believed the thing would not have happened if I hadn't placed the call to my uncle. Ironically, it was out of concern for Mom that I had made the call to begin with. It was just the kind of quandary to cause a 9-year-old boy to question his self-worth, and it consumed me. The ordeal left me in a perpetual state of guilt, often over things I'd had no hand in bringing about. This was to become a lifelong pattern as I lived with a sense of irrevocable debt.

shattered

Grandma sensed the turmoil I was in. One night, after I had brushed my teeth and changed into my pajamas, I lay in the dark, waiting for Grandma to come tuck me in. It was only about a week after we had put Mom in the ground. Grandma came in and sat on the end of the bed.

"Are you okay?" She patted my leg through the covers.

"Is it okay to cry now?" I asked.

"Oh, honey, yes, you can!" she said, still patting my leg. It was all I needed. The tears flowed freely in an explosion of pent-up grief that, according to Grandma, lasted for hours. All I remember was her giving me permission to cry. It was Grandma who sat there with me long into the night. When I woke the next morning, the sheets were still damp from my tears.

❧❧❧

The next several years were productive and hopeful. My schooling and social life ran their course on an even keel. After spending several months at Grandma's house, Uncle Wade asked me if I would like to come live on his dairy farm. I became part of the family, learned the farming business and rose at 4 a.m. for chores with the rest of the house. I worked like I was possessed, and I was in the best shape of my life. I had my own John Deere tractor to use, and I put an incalculable number of miles on it as I went all over the farm about my work.

The years on Uncle Wade's farm helped me to mature quickly. I grew in both stature and physical strength, finished high school and became self-sufficient. However, even as many good things were being added to my life, the specter of calamity and violence would follow me for years to come.

When I was 12, I lost Aunt Sherri and Uncle Don when their vehicle was struck by a train. When I was 23, for reasons that were never known, Uncle Jack shot his wife and stepdaughter, then turned the gun on himself. The gruesome task of cleaning up the remains of Uncle Jack's suicide fell to me and a close family friend, Reed. The experience haunts me to this day.

Two years later, my cousin Mandy died when her husband accidentally backed over her with his tractor. She was four months pregnant when it happened. Mandy had been like a sister to me as we grew up in the Treasure Valley together. After she died, I was troubled for many years because I had never told her that I loved her. The experience stamped into me the hard lesson that we should tell our loved ones what they mean to us, since we have no way of knowing how much time we will enjoy with them.

These experiences, particularly seeing the aftermath of Uncle Jack's suicide, stamped a dark posture inside me. In a way I never examined directly, I lived with the idea that violence and tragedy were my unshakeable inheritance. I saw calamity descending perpetually, which drove me into a frenzy trying to outrun it. I don't fully understand how I lived with the knowledge that violent death had killed eight of my family members in 15 years, including my only parent. It was settled into my mind as a young boy that the world was almost ravenous in its brutality. The fact had been driven home when I was 9 years old watching my mother put a butcher knife in her belly. These grisly events were just more of the same, and they drove me to try to control everything — most of all, my own emotions — so that life's cruelties couldn't penetrate. Anger was the exception. Not only was it perfectly acceptable for a man to show anger, it was useful as an energy source. To my way of thinking, it was a just and fitting way of regarding the foul world that had taken so much from me. I cut my losses and cultivated my natural strengths. But as my unyielding disposition toppled all kinds of barriers in my life and work, my own sorrow imposed a far greater obstacle, and it lay untouched like an infection in my gut for many years.

᭡᭡᭡

I was 23 when I met and married my first wife, Belinda. I was earning a considerable wage working in a silver mine in Southern Idaho when a mutual friend introduced us. Before I knew it, I was falling for her. She was intelligent and attractive, and her family liked me from the start. We said our vows, and soon we were moving around the country wherever my mining employment took us. I was highly skilled and fiercely ambitious, so I was seldom without work. Within a few years, Belinda had given birth to two boys, Zane and

beauty for ashes

Samuel. To celebrate our second wedding anniversary, Belinda and I flew to Sydney, Australia, to attend the 1988 World's Fair. It was a time of optimism in my life and marriage, all the more exhilarating for the opportunity to visit a country bursting with exotic animals and beautiful scenery. Everything was new — especially the surprise that was waiting for me at the end of the trip.

We were just walking off an extravagant meal of barbecued shrimp and roasted potatoes when, quite by accident, we came upon an enormous Catholic cathedral. The beauty of it began to cause a stirring inside me while we were still at a distance. It was like a castle, its spires rising up to impale the sky. When I saw it, my breath caught in my throat. It was as if the surrounding buildings disappeared, and the cathedral was ensconced on a high hill, with nothing around it but lush green trees and the sparkling seacoast.

The building was girded on every side by stonework — great slabs of jagged slate laid into its walls like pieces of a vast jigsaw puzzle. The sun leapt off the panes of its stained-glass windows as we moved. Every inch of the building was scrubbed clean and perfectly arranged. Even the grass marched right up to the stone, its expanse broken only by a wide cobblestone path that wound through it to the entrance.

The moment we entered the building, something unfamiliar moved through the entire upper portion of my body. I realized a few moments later that what I was feeling was peace. Then I stopped breathing when we

shattered

stepped from the foyer into the sanctuary. I looked up and up, my eyes finally finding the domed ceiling, which was at least 300 feet above our heads, supported by arches upon arches, all rising majestically to an impossible height. The space in the sanctuary was gargantuan, and every square foot sparkled, from the marble floor up to the gilded dome of the ceiling, where narrow arched windows permitted the sunlight to stream down in shining rays that looked like the fingers of God.

I felt a strange pressure in my chest when I saw the Stations of the Cross. I had never seen the crucifixion of Christ depicted so respectfully before. There was a reverence here that was palpable. No one was speaking. The visitors sat in the pews or stood in a contemplative, prayerful posture. The only sound was an organ playing softly. Something inside me broke, and in seconds my cheeks were wet with tears. I felt Belinda's hand on my shoulder.

"What's wrong, sweetheart?" she said, and the gentle compassion in her voice made me cry harder. I couldn't answer her. I was sobbing now. My whole body shook with tremors that seemed to grow more intense by the second. I put my face in my hands and squinched my eyes shut, struggling to stop crying. There was no way I could sit here in a public building and blubber like this. But I couldn't stop. There was something happening deep inside me, in a place I hadn't even known existed. Some internal door had been opened, and I was pushing with all my strength, but I couldn't shut it again.

beauty for ashes

I'd grown up believing that men weren't supposed to cry, certainly not around other people, and preferably not at all. Furthermore, I was afraid of losing control of my emotions. Through all the grotesque things I had witnessed, I had responded to the world's assaults by struggling for control. It was how I dealt with the state of near-panic I had lived with for as long as I could remember. My constant companion was a fear of some unknown catastrophe, like an emergency that never got resolved, but with all the attendant responsibility to act. My fear spoke of an impending disaster I couldn't fix, but I went on running myself ragged just the same. And I refused to cry.

Now, however, I couldn't stop crying. The surge of tears went on for 30 minutes or more as I stood in the cathedral. The experience was at once fearful and splendid.

On a level that was deeper than language and mental comprehension, something was drawing me away from the carefully arranged life I had striven to maintain, a nameless voice that promised the peace and rest I had craved for so long. However, I was held back by an inability to understand what had happened — and to control it. Each time I walked into a church after that day, I felt the same sensation of being swept away. So I avoided churches altogether.

ॐॐॐ

shattered

In the meantime, more tumult was on the way. Belinda called me at work out of the blue one morning in 1991.

"I'm leaving. The boys are at the neighbors."

"What?! Why?"

"I just have to go."

"You have to give me a better reason than *that*. What's wrong?"

"I can't talk about it. I just need to leave."

I couldn't get her to change her mind or even tell me why she was leaving. I made some initial adjustments, including moving with my boys into a camper for a time. I strained to meet my work obligations while caring for an infant and a toddler.

The divorce left me in an emotional desert, contemplating suicide. It was more devastating than anything I had gone through before. I had given my heart to Belinda; she had become part of my identity. Her abandonment eviscerated me. I was inches away from taking my life. All the violent death and suicide that had coalesced around my family pressed on me with a fresh agony. I could almost hear my departed family members calling me to follow them out.

In the end, I decided I couldn't subject my boys to the same thing Mom had done to me. One way or another, I would have to walk through this conflagration that had been visited on me. I staggered through the next few years, trying to understand why Belinda had done it. *What could be so wrong with me that she had been driven to desert me and our boys?* I wondered. No answers came.

beauty for ashes

The difficulty of working and raising my boys in a vacuum was ironically what kept me alive. However inadequate I was, I had to go to work. My little boys, Zane and Samuel, looked up at me every morning, needing me, loving me and expecting me to come through for them. My work and my boys became my world.

I gradually found my stride again, though I remained unfulfilled. My stand against the world survived years of fruitless searching that continued even as I bent to my work and looked after my boys, who grew like weeds.

Many years later, after I had remarried, a chance conversation with a coworker brought my attention back to the cathedral in Sydney. (Ralph had always had a knack for getting me onto squishy subjects, but I could never be angry at him for it.) Although the experience had been unquestionably important and spectacular, I always felt a little bothered whenever I opened it up. The reason, I suppose, was that it was unfinished business. There was a call to action in it that I was avoiding.

Ralph and I were sitting in the cab of my pickup eating ham sandwiches and potato salad when the conversation turned to God. I began relating the details of my "Sydney adventure," as I had come to call it. I described the cathedral and the colossal sanctuary, the sense of deep reverence I had felt, the Stations of the Cross and the crying spell that had lasted for half an hour.

"I still have no idea what in the world went on in there." I paused to take a bite of ham sandwich. "It's the strangest thing that's ever happened to me."

Ralph smiled. After a pause, he asked, "You don't know what that was?"

"No."

"Would you come to church with me?"

I shook my head as I spooned some potato salad into my mouth. "I'm not sure I'm ready for that. You have no idea how intense that experience was. And the same thing has happened every time I've gone into a church since then."

"What's so bad about that?" he asked, chuckling.

I couldn't come up with an answer.

The following Sunday, I pulled into the parking lot of Ralph's church, a large red and grey wooden structure that sat next to a roiling creek. I met Ralph in the vestibule at 9:30, as we'd planned. I tensed up as we walked into the sanctuary, bracing for another emotional wave. However, I was surprised to feel a calmness settle over me.

We got through the music and half of the sermon when the pastor's words began to hit me between the eyes. He could have been speaking directly to me.

"What are we to conclude about the state of this world? Has God abandoned this place? Is he some cosmic psychopath, chuckling to himself as he watches when parents kill their children, when teenagers die from drug overdoses, when people wither away in cancer wards or convalescent hospitals, forgotten by their families, when distraught, lonely souls put shotguns in their mouths? Perhaps he has no feelings. Or maybe he doesn't have the power to eliminate evil. Maybe the devil is God's ugly twin, and all of human history has been a long wrestling match between the two of them, with all of us getting ground to bits in the middle.

"No!" the pastor thundered with such sudden force that I almost jumped in the pew. "The suffering and tragedy in our lives is God's gift to us. That's right! *Gift!* Not a curse. Our curse is that we are all satisfied to do our own thing and leave God out of the equation. God sends upheaval into our lives to get our attention! What choice does he have? We're too busy amassing fortunes, building bigger houses, taking vacations, fiddling with our Androids, filling our lives with everything but him.

"C.S. Lewis wrote, 'God whispers to us in our pleasures, speaks in our conscience, but shouts in our pains: It is his megaphone to rouse a deaf world.' Which of us can say we don't need a bit of rousing, that we're doing just fine on our own? There might be a few of us, but I'm guessing most of you out there will admit that you need something more than CNN, Facebook and Internet pornography.

"Who do you think made all this? Who put all of us here on this lush, gorgeous planet, with a billion things for us to enjoy? How is it that we ignore the greatest gift of all — Christ himself, who gave himself willingly so each of us could experience this God, an ocean of love that calls untiringly to us. Don't leave here without answering him! Come down to the front and meet him. He's waiting for you!"

I was weeping long before the pastor had finished

speaking. I walked down to the platform at the front, knelt in front of 200 strangers and gave my life to Christ.

Ralph was beaming as we emerged from the church, talking. "This was set into motion a long time ago. That was God loving on you in that cathedral, Joseph."

"I know. I can't believe it took me so long to see that. I'm starting to believe that it was God who got me through all those hard years, before I even knew he was real."

"That wouldn't surprise me at all," he agreed.

I launched myself vigorously into Bible study and church attendance. I wanted to learn everything I could. In my reading and in discussions about the meaning of Christ's redemption, I was driven by a desire to know more about the process of change that had begun in me in the cathedral. The life of a believer that I was now living was a kind of formalization. My mind and personal habits were catching up with my heart.

I found myself wanting to please God in the matters of my speech and inner attitudes. I had a long daily commute, and I used the time to listen to recorded Christian programs on the radio. As all this played out, I began to see entire pieces of my life come together in ways I couldn't have dreamed of.

During this time, I learned that my lifelong friend, Troy, whom I had known since we were each in the fourth grade, had also become a believer in Christ and was struggling through his own Christian walk. We had survived many of the same things: broken families, experimentation with drinking and drugs, romantic misadventures. In the most dramatic parallel of all, he had lost his father to suicide.

When my second marriage failed, Troy kept me company, as he has done so often through our decades of friendship. These were years of trial and error, tumult in my family and struggles in my spiritual life. I was more surprised than anyone by the arrival of my present wife, Kristy, who came along after I had already resigned myself to being a bachelor. Our marriage has been a succession of trials, like everything else in the past 10 years.

When Kristy and I began looking for a church together, we went through the yellow pages, of all things. But God works in mysterious ways. We found Christian Life Fellowship, walked into the building and immediately spotted our future pastor, Doug, who waved from the other side of the foyer and called, "Welcome home!"

Whether the greeting was prophetic or wishful, it was accurate. Kristy and I discovered that this was the same church where our daughter, Stephanie, was already attending the youth group with a friend. As we began attending in earnest, we found the pastor to be sincere and passionate. His honesty about many of his own failings has been instrumental in helping me contend with mine. The church emphasizes healing and prayer and works to equip its members through Biblical teaching — which was precisely what I was looking to accomplish in my life and marriage. Pastor Doug became one of the most influential people in my life, past and present. In spite of shepherding a congregation of 300 people, he made time on several occasions to provide counseling as Kristy and I worked through our trials.

"He saved our marriage," Kristy declared memorably once, as we were sharing our story with a friend from Portland, Oregon, in an impromptu phone conversation recently.

Indeed, "impromptu" has so often turned into "divine" when I have examined things in retrospect. It is the story of my life.

One day not long ago, I spotted one of my coworkers trudging out to his truck at noon.

"Luke!" I called, to stop him so I could catch up. "Where are you headed?" I skidded to a stop on the gravel.

"Home."

"In the middle of the day?"

He shrugged. Suddenly, it came to me in a flash that he was planning to hurt himself.

"Hey, look," I said, "it's lunchtime. I'm hungry. Why don't we go get burgers and fries around the corner? I'm buying."

He shook his head. "No, I've got someplace I need to be."

"C'mon, it's only 30 minutes. Whatever it is will wait that long, right?"

Finally he consented, but 10 minutes later, we were doing the same awkward dance in the diner while our burger baskets grew cold in front of us.

"Luke, something's really bothering you. It's obvious. Tell me what's going on."

beauty for ashes

After more prodding, he spoke. "My wife is seeking a divorce. She's been gone out of the house for two months. I haven't seen my daughter the whole time." He struggled to hold back tears.

I nodded. "I know the pain of divorce. Been there twice."

"It's my own fault. I've been drinking up a storm. I haven't been a proper husband or father. I've made a mess of everything."

"And now you're about to do something irreversible."

He looked up at me suspiciously. "That's none of your d*** business."

"Maybe not. But I can see it in your eyes. You'll be making a huge mistake."

"That's not for you to say!" he said angrily.

"It's not?" I felt emotions well up in me. I breathed in sharply and reflected on my worst memory.

"I watched my own mother put a carving knife up to the hilt in her belly. You need to hear how much I've suffered because she did that. What you're planning is the height of selfishness!"

"How can you judge me? You don't know what I've been through."

I leaned in close. "You don't know what *I've* been through. You think I haven't wanted to say goodbye? My mother committed suicide. My father deserted me. Many of my family members have been killed. I've gone to more funerals than most teenagers have been to rock concerts. I treated two wives as well as I knew how, but after a second divorce, I was all alone in my 40s, an angry man. But I decided a long time ago I wasn't going to subject my sons to what my mother did to me. Now you're in the same situation. You have no idea how much sorrow you'll bring down on your little girl's head if you do this. You need to think of her, not yourself."

Luke said nothing for a long time. I sat across from him and waited in silence. Then, finally, he let out a great heaving sigh. "Okay. You're right." His words were barely audible.

I reached across the table and grabbed his arm. "I want you to promise me."

"I promise. I'm not doing it."

"All right. If I've earned any credibility with you, take this scripture and run with it: 'And we know that in God, all things work together for the good of those who love him, who have been called according to his purpose.' Romans 8:28, that's my life verse. I have it on speed dial." I tapped my temple. "You've been through some awful things, but if you'll trust God, he's promised to replace your pain with blessings."

I saw Luke coming and going after that and often felt a thrill that I had been placed in his path that day.

I have had so many of these encounters that I've lost count. Even as God uses me to bring other people back (usually from near-suicide or drunken ruin), he is having an ongoing dialogue with me. It's as though he is saying to me over and over, *You can trust my promises. I haven't wasted an ounce of your pain, and I never will.*

beauty for ashes

And so he hasn't. The blessings I've been given far outweigh the pain I've endured. I like to call it beauty for ashes.

the will to fly
The Story of Ashley
Written by Lori McClure

I brought the axe down hard, felt the satisfaction of split wood and tried to push aside the events of last night. Every ounce of energy poured into cracking that timber, into pretending nothing had changed since yesterday. But my world had changed. Nothing was the same. Until last night, I was just one of the guys. In a matter of moments, Jason, my boss, ruined it all. Now, words rang in my head of the boys congratulating me as if I'd won a prize. But Jason was no prize. Last night left me numb as my mind replayed what I fought hard to forget with every swing of the axe ...

୰୰୰

The clock inched past 10 p.m., and I was more than ready to get back on the road for the 45-minute drive home. Six o'clock was an early start, and I'd worked in the field all day. My night was spent cleaning the boss' home, but I was thankful for the extra money. Every penny would help me pay for college.

I finished the job as Jason came in the main entrance, which happened to be a sliding glass door located in his bedroom. I was on my way out when he stopped to pay me. He came in for a hug, a strange way for a boss to end the day. He took a $100 bill and reached for my shirt to place it inside. I batted him away, nervously made a joke and wanted nothing more than to leave the awkward interchange for the safety of my car.

"I need to go. My mom's waiting for me. I should leave."

"No, you're not leaving." Jason positioned himself between me and the door. He stood uncomfortably close. I pushed him away, but for him it seemed a game. He returned my reluctance with more force, pushed me back so that I fell hard onto his bed.

Anger rose up within me as I fought to get my feet back on solid ground.

"Let me go! I'm leaving!" But I wasn't leaving. He was too strong. This couldn't be happening. Terror came dressed in a green Element t-shirt and blue jeans.

❧❧❧

The pale baby-yellow walls seemed an odd fit for a room witness to such darkness only a few moments earlier. The scent of lavender carpet cleaning powder hung in the air, too weak to cover the musty odor embedded into the very walls of his place. I hurried to the bathroom and locked the door, feeling rushed to be rid of him. I wanted to shower, to scrub away every trace of him — every evidence of what just happened. Guilt covered me like a wet blanket. Was this my fault? I hurried to get dressed and made my way to the sliding glass door.

"I'll need you at work tomorrow," he said casually, as if we'd been hanging out playing Scrabble or checkers. I left without a word.

But I showed up again the next day because I needed to work. College would come at the end of the month. My musical education waited for me in Seattle. And no one and nothing would stop me from going, not even Jason.

I knew Jason had been talking as soon as I got to work. The guys congratulated me as if last night had been mutual, and embarrassment enveloped me. I said nothing. In shock, I focused on work. I just had to make it to the end of the month, and I'd be free.

Jason peacocked his way toward me, and when I caught his eye, he winked. The strangeness of it all gripped my insides with fear. I didn't want to get in trouble. I had no desire to get Jason in trouble. I just wanted it all to go away. My mom was already unhappy about the long hours I worked, and I knew that if I confided in her, my college future would be in jeopardy. Mom would immediately pull me out of the situation, and I wouldn't have the money to go off to college. I was making more than $100 a day. Without this money, there would be no college for me. Thoughts swirled in my head and solidified the awful truth that I couldn't tell anyone about what happened. Everyone thought I was his girlfriend now. In the eyes of my coworkers, my role at work was changing.

The pressure cooker that became my life overnight was sealed. Jason and I were together. I *was* his girlfriend. I couldn't stop the inevitable, but I knew the end of the month would bring relief. I would move on with my life, and the uncomfortable truth of what happened that night would be left behind.

అా అా అా

I made it! Seattle and Shoreline Community College greeted me. Even though I had no family or friends in the area, the thought of my 22-hour course load as a vocal performance major energized me. My dreams were unfolding. Musically, I would find my way.

It was hard to believe how far I'd come. Here I was, an outdoorsy Montana girl who had made my way to the city to chase my dreams. I felt proud. I was ready to shake away my past and push ahead to new beginnings.

On the first day of audio engineering class, excitement buzzed in the air around me. My professor asked, "Is there anything new you want to try now that you're in college?" My heart jumped at the possibility.

"I'd like to try singing jazz," I piped in.

"Well, Dave is a jazz guitarist, so maybe he could hook you up with some opportunities." And with that, I had my first friend in Seattle.

అా అా అా

Dave quickly became a fixture in my life. Our friendship was easy, and he came over after class every day to hang out. It was nice to have a friend. Even my landlord got to know him, as often as he came around. I started to trust him.

"Hey, Ashley, a group of us are going to see Jason Mraz in Spokane, and I've got an extra ticket. I can drive, and we'll even get two rooms — one for the guys, one for the girls. You wanna go?"

"Sure!" It did sound fun, and he was taking care of everything, so why not?

We arrived in Spokane for the concert, and no one else was there. No group waited to meet us. There weren't two hotel rooms. My stomach dropped. I was in the middle of nowhere with no one to call for help that wasn't hours away. I could get through this. I would be fine.

"We need to get another hotel room." The answer was simple.

"You can't get another hotel room because you don't have a credit card, do you?"

"No, I don't."

"Look, it's not a big deal, Ashley. You can sleep in the room with me, and it'll be fine. Let's just go to the concert and worry about it later."

So we did. But when we returned, the reality of my situation hit hard. Here I was, in the middle of nowhere in a cheap hotel room with an ugly floral-printed polyester bedspread and no way out. Within moments, my life became a complete replay of what happened with Jason. Dave made an advance. I denied him. He persisted with force. I fought back, even screamed thinking surely someone would hear. He still won. His hand covered my mouth as he gave a final warning. "You won't tell anyone."

Blame washed over me in fresh waves, and only one conclusion sank in deep: I was a whore. I had been with two guys in two months' time. Unwanted as the acts were, the common denominator was me. This is all I am. This is all I will ever be: the girl guys only want to sleep with. That's me. How did this become my story, my destiny, to be used up in this way?

I lay on my side of the bed for the rest of the night wide-awake, freaking out internally. Even though I had lost the extra weight I carried in my early high school years, the insecurities remained and raged within me. I still felt uncomfortable in my own skin. I missed the innocence of high school boyfriends — of times when holding hands was enough and when a soft kiss satisfied. Now, I felt dirty, unclean and trapped yet again.

The next morning, I stayed quiet. I just had to make it back to school with the least amount of trouble possible. Dave acted nonchalant, as if we'd had a normal overnight trip. I let music build a wall between us as we drove home.

The Mars Volta provided the soundtrack to my confused life as I sat on the passenger side and stared out the window. Nausea rocked my body with each dissonant chord. "Banana Pancakes" and "Bubbly Toes" played through the speakers, and the beachy vibe did nothing but sear an unwanted connection in my soul between Jack Johnson and this horrendous weekend.

Plans formed in my mind. I'd keep my distance. I lived alone, so I could lock the gate and avoid him. I'd sit as far away from him as possible in class. I could do this. I was strong. I would deal with this on my own.

But my plans were weak. He showed up everywhere: at my house, at class — anywhere I was he found a way to be there, too. To make things worse, Dave decided to rewrite the story — my story. He told everyone we were together. Strength eluded me, and I couldn't fight him or his persistence. I didn't know how to get away from him, and I didn't have the resolve to let the truth be known. Now everyone thought we were in a relationship. It didn't help that we shared two classes together. How could I be rid of him? I saw no way out with our school schedules constantly throwing us together.

One of our classes included involvement in a bar band. He was the guitarist, I the vocalist. We'd learn cover songs and perform them around downtown Seattle. I lost myself in the music, but sometimes the discord of my emotions broke through. When I sang The Eagles' "Heartache Tonight," I'd try to lose myself in my musical safe haven, but with every guitar harmony riffing through the song, with every strum, my irritation increased. I couldn't get away from him.

అ అ అ

The harder I tried, the worse things became. Dave's controlling ways escalated. When I expressed my discomfort with our situation, the words left my mouth and dropped heavy to the ground as they met his reply.

shattered

"No one else is going to love you. You're dirty now. Don't you know I'm the only one that even wants you, so why would you try to be with anybody else?" His mental games trapped me in a web, and I couldn't break free. The more I fought, the more entangled I became. Whatever he told me to do, I did. It seemed to make my life easier in the short term to obey.

One day the abuse took a nasty turn. He still lived with his parents, and he took me to see them. His mother sat in the room with us, while Dave sat next to me. I got up from my seat, and he pulled me back down.

"Where are you going?" I assumed he was being playful as he started to tickle me. I batted him away so I could get up again. Out of nowhere, he punched me in the stomach three times as hard as he could while his mom watched. Then he got up and walked away as I sat with the wind knocked out of me, appalled and in shock.

"Well, that wasn't very nice," his mom said nonchalantly.

Dave had grabbed me by the arm hard enough to leave bruises more than once to get what he wanted from me. I couldn't believe he had punched me. And in front of his *mom*. He was more messed up than I thought. Fear grew stronger inside of me as I tried to process the position I now found myself in. Terror squeezed me like a vice grip. I had no words for the rest of our time with his parents. I endured dinner and a movie with his family in silence.

The night air wrapped heavy around me as I opened the door to his navy-blue Subaru. I slid into the passenger seat and watched him climb into the car in his stupid brown boat shoes with the tan laces I hated. Anger welled up in me. How did I, a Montana cowgirl, end up here with this abusive city boy? Why had I let him manipulate me into being with him? How did I even end up agreeing to go to his parents' house in the first place? I was livid.

"What the h*** is your problem?" I finally exploded and shot angry words in his direction. "Do you even realize what you just did — what just happened?"

"What do you mean?" he said calmly.

My eyes widened in disbelief. "What do I mean? You punched me. You physically punched me as hard as you could in my stomach!"

"No, I didn't. I don't remember doing that." He denied it again and again.

"You're crazy if you think I believe you don't remember punching me," I said in disbelief.

"I swear, I don't remember hitting you because I didn't hit you." Was he psychotic?

The next day, I lifted my shirt and showed him the bruises. "You did this to me." I pointed to the dark circles where his fist had slammed against me.

"No, I didn't do that to you, and I'm sorry you think I did." He was too calm.

I was beginning to understand what he was capable of and just how unstable he was, but what could I do about it? I knew I needed to get rid of him, but I didn't know how.

shattered

ର୍ଜ୍ୟର୍ଜ୍

Alcohol added to our problems and became an excuse for me not to care so much about the chaos of our dysfunction. The band often threw parties after our performances. Dave started pressuring me to drink at the parties, and I gave in.

Alcohol provided a means to get through the times he took all he wanted from me — the times he used me up, even though I didn't want him to. The less I resisted, the fewer bruises I received. Alcohol dulled my senses while he had his way with me. I'd zone out when he took advantage of me. I'd stare at the old-school gray metal heater and memorize its accordion-like folds, its long back cord. I'd estimate its height, maybe three feet? I'd focus on the four wheels it stood on for easy movement. That heater kept my mind busy, kept me sane in an insane situation.

Even though I'd found a new way to cope, I still wanted out. I went home for Christmas break more determined than ever to end things with Dave. I told his friend Eric about my plans, about how unhappy I was and about how Dave was not right for me.

"Ashley, you can't do that! He loves you. He's obsessed with you. You can't do that to him. You'll break his heart. It would hurt him more than you know." His persistence made me uncomfortable.

"No, you don't understand. He doesn't love me. He doesn't treat me well. That's the problem." My mind flashed to every bruise, to every foul word Dave had ever uttered to me.

"Well, give me an example." But I couldn't. My tongue felt paralyzed, and the words wouldn't come. "Just wait, Ashley, until you get back to Seattle. Just wait, and see how it goes. Maybe things will get better." So I listened to Eric, and I waited to end things with Dave.

∂∂∂∂

Things only got worse. Between the alcohol and the abuse, our relationship continued its negative spiral. We were midway through the spring semester, and Dave wanted to go to a party his friend was throwing. I wasn't comfortable with the idea. I couldn't shake the cryptic feeling in the pit of my stomach.

"I don't really want to go. I won't know anyone." I knew resistance was futile.

"You'll meet Renee, and you'll have fun with her. We don't have to stay long, but we're going." And with that, I let him lead the dance of our lives yet again, even though he was spinning me out of control.

As we drove up to the apartment, I took a deep breath, and he told me how it was going to be.

"Go hang out with Renee. Whatever she drinks, you drink." The easy way was to listen — to do what I was told. We walked inside. The small apartment was filled to capacity. The DJ, with his eyes lined and his long jet-black hair swept to one side, had his gear set up in front of the

TV blasting dance music. I made my way through the predominantly male crowd to find Renee and follow my orders for the night.

She took me under her crazy wing immediately. "Hey, let's do some shots!" Bodies pressed into the kitchen counter as shots were poured for consumption in quick succession. Random cheers wafted through the air.

"Do another one! Do another one!" Within a matter of 30 minutes, I had downed at least eight shots of 100-proof gas station vodka.

By 11:30, we were in the car. I tried to talk to my sister on the phone through the haze my brain was shrouded in. I looked over to see Dave laughing at me, and my focus turned to the streetlights. I watched through the window as each one passed, followed them as if it were my job to concentrate on their passing halos.

ॐॐॐ

I woke up to find myself in the shower, covered in nothing but black vomit as cold water rained down upon me. Dave sat across from me, watching me.

"What's going on?" I managed to push the words out.

"You had way too much to drink." Excruciating pain shot through every part of my body, but I felt disconnected from the experience. I had no control.

"What time is it?"

"It's 2 o'clock in the morning. We got home a little before midnight, and you've been like this ever since." My body heaved again, emptying what was left of my stomach's contents.

"I need to go to the hospital."

"I'm not taking you to the hospital, Ashley. We're underage, and if my parents find out, I'll be in trouble."

I knew we were underage. *But what if I'm not okay?* I thought. *What if I'm going to die? What if I've had way too much to drink? What's going to happen to me?* My mind spun with questions I couldn't answer. And then all went black again.

☙☙☙

The second time I woke up, I found myself in bed with uncontrollable tremors. I could see Dave beside me staring at the TV.

I managed to mumble, "I need to go to the hospital. I'm not okay."

"I told you I'm not taking you to the hospital." Again, he was too calm.

I reached for my cell phone and called my mom who was a nine-hour drive away.

"Ashley, are you okay?" I could hear Mom's voice on the line.

"No, I'm not. Mom, I think I have alcohol poisoning, and I need to go to the hospital."

"Are you by yourself? Where are you?" Her concerned voice sounded so far away.

"I'm at home. Dave's here, but he won't take me ..."

shattered

Before I could finish, Dave ripped the phone from my hands and took the battery out of it.

He looked me straight in the eye and said it again. "We're not going to the hospital."

I started to cry, and he grabbed my face. "Your pupils are so small, like smaller than the tip of a pencil." He said it as a casual observer, and reality settled in hard. I was going to die in this room with a psychotic boyfriend by my side.

Thoughts swirled one after the other. *Why am I even alive? Why? I can't even call my mom for help. I'm stuck here. This is it, and I'm ready to go. Look at the mess my life has become. No one's going to want me after being used and abused. I am worthless. I want to die. Just let me die.*

For the next few hours, my mind pushed and pulled in and out of reality, but somehow I survived the night. *How did I get in this awful mess? How did I get so far away from the girl I used to be?* My mind was reeling.

❧❧❧

I grew up in a typical American family. We lived near Glacier National Park in Montana. My mother was a stay-at-home mom, and my father's work kept him preoccupied, so the majority of the time, it was only me, Mom and my younger sister. Dad's work schedule took a toll on everyone, and my parents eventually separated.

When divorce permanently split our family, I was left

with a deep unhappiness that resulted in depression. Dad was always traveling for work, and by the time he decided to stop traveling and focus on our family, I wasn't interested in spending time with him anymore. When he proclaimed to us that he asked God to change him and began attending church, it felt like a manipulative plan to keep our family together. He became someone I didn't recognize.

At first, my sister and I alternated weeks between parents. Every Monday marked a new home for the week, and the instability pushed me further into depression. I announced that I wanted to live with my mom permanently, and my dad agreed based on one condition: that I would meet him at church on Wednesday nights. I did so reluctantly.

One night, my father suggested I go to a youth worship service hosted by our church. I loved music, so I threw on my favorite jeans and went. The vibe was more like a concert than a church service, which spoke to my passions. The room was dark except for the stage lighting that left a blue hue dusted over the stage and crowd. The music drew me in immediately as the worship leader's voice sang passionately, "… let us rejoice at the foot of the cross, we can be free and give glory to God …" She sang with a palpable focus and intensity I craved for my own life. The music and words seemed to hold a meaning I'd never noticed before. An ache grew inside of me as I soaked in the comfort that dripped from her song. I could feel her words piercing me. Then someone else came to the microphone and started to speak of God's love. Words penetrated my heart with a truth I had never been able to see before now.

The youth pastor stepped up, and his words echoed through the room of 200 teenagers. "God is our father, and though you may not have a perfect earthly father's love, God is the perfect father you're looking for." The words hit me hard. Tears flowed as I dropped to my knees with my heart opened wide.

I realized that I had associated God with the hurt I felt during my parents' divorce. My dad had turned to God, and it somehow felt manipulative and hurtful. But now, blame and anger melted away as the idea of God began to separate from the hurt of the relationship I lacked with my father. God was real, and he loved me so much he sent his son, Jesus, to die for *me*. He defeated death and lived again for *me*. He wanted to rescue me from the mess I was trapped in.

"Can I pray for you?" A girl had seen my tears and approached me. Even though the whole experience was strange, I wanted her to pray for me, and I let her. When she finished, she asked, "Are you saved?" I knew I wasn't.

"No." The experience was so new to me, but I wanted more of everything I felt bubbling up inside of me.

"Do you want to be?" Her presence was sure and enthusiastic, and I was ready for all she had to offer. I wanted Jesus to save me from all the chaos. I wanted to feel whole inside instead of endlessly unhappy. I was experiencing what my dad had described a few months before. It was not about manipulation, I realized, it was about restoration. I was ready to give my life to God.

"Sure." And with that single syllable, my beginning with God happened. The heaviness I carried deep in my soul was gone. Hope poured in, and I felt the perpetual weight of darkness I'd been carrying lift. God was real to me for the first time. I didn't feel alone, and I knew he would never leave me. I didn't have to feel alone ever again.

❧❧❧

Time, and all that life brought, forged a distance between God and me. I tried to ignore it, but I could feel the distance growing.

Looking back, I could see how I started hiding from God on that awful night with Jason. A chasm formed that I didn't know how to bridge. Even now, waking up after the worst night of my life, I couldn't believe I was alive. Why did God let me live?

My body hurt in every way possible, but it was the day of the Super Bowl, and Dave expected me to go with him to his parents' house. After calling my mother and downplaying the previous night's fiasco, I braced for the day ahead. I didn't know if I could make it through, but I knew what was expected of me.

"You know, kid, you don't look so good." His dad wrapped his arm around my shoulder.

"Well, I don't feel very good."

shattered

"Dave told me he had to come pick you up from a party last night. Have you learned your lesson?"

"Yeah." It would do no good to explain.

"You probably won't be drinking that much again, huh?"

Dave always twisted the truth. He had been with me at the party, but he made sure to protect his own reputation for his parents. He could say whatever he wanted. I was too tired to care. While football played, I had plenty of time to think about how wearisome my life had become. I had plenty of time to soak in my thoughts and contemplate why I didn't want to live anymore.

ลิลิลิ

I didn't think things could get worse with Dave, but I was wrong.

His demands became more bizarre as he forced me into uncomfortable and inappropriate situations he would later deny or blame on alcohol consumption. When he denied sleeping with my friend, I saw my way out. I confronted him, and he refused to admit what I knew was true — what I'd seen with my own eyes. For the first time, I felt empowered when our fight ended because I made it clear I was done. I couldn't continue in our relationship. Maybe I could do this. Maybe I could get away from him. Lyrics spun in my head, and I rushed to write them down.

the will to fly

... Cause here I am again, home alone again
Soberin' up after drownin' in your love
You made me such a fool, and I don't know what to do
To get myself over you
So I'm sippin' on a glass of my cheap wine, prayin' in
the morning I'll be fine
For as they say, this, too, shall pass, this, too, shall pass
in time

Well, I've been cryin' for days hung-over with a
headache
From thinking of you and all that wasn't true
Now I'm watchin' it all pass away with time ...

With the song of my heart on paper, resolve came. I could be free of him. I wouldn't let him have me anymore. But the respite only lasted one weekend. He returned on Monday to fix what he'd done wrong. At first, he said he wanted me in his life — that he was sorry. It was a normal conversation, but it only took moments to end in the same mentally, emotionally and physically destructive pattern that characterized our relationship.

My feeling of empowerment was gone. His obsession, his control and his abuse ensnared me.

But school demands continued. Exams and classes didn't stop because Dave tormented me. Forward seemed the only way through.

ॐॐॐ

shattered

The band had an outdoor performance in the college courtyard after which I'd made plans with a friend to avoid Dave. As we tore down the gear, he approached me.

"I don't want you going out with Lauren." His eyes already seemed wild.

"Dave, these are the plans I've made, and I'm not changing them." I wrapped the equipment cords around and around in my hands methodically, trying to stay calm.

"You're my girlfriend, and I don't want you to go." His barely controlled anger brewed just below the surface.

"I know, but I made plans. I still have friends I want to see and hang out with, Dave." He grabbed my arm hard, the first time he'd ever done so in public, and my heart skipped a beat.

"Listen to me. You're my girlfriend, and you're going to do what I say." His teeth clenched, but I continued wrapping the cords, standing my ground.

"No, Dave, I'm sorry. I'm going to go hang out with my friends." I stayed calm, but he started to lose what little control he had left. He grabbed my arm, pulled me close and sandwiched me between him and the wall.

"You're disrespecting me, and I won't have it. You're going to hang out with me because you do what I tell you to do!"

Jackie, a sound engineer, saw the mess I was in and came to my rescue. She tapped Dave on the shoulder and said, "Excuse me, but you don't talk to a lady like that." Dave looked at her, looked at me and stormed off.

"Are you okay?" Jackie was the first to see what I'd

managed to keep hidden. "How long has this been going on?"

I appreciated her concern, but unable to speak honestly, I brushed her off. "Oh, it's okay. He's just upset. It's fine. I'm fine." The looped cords still hung in my hands, grounding me.

"Well, you know you don't deserve that. I'm glad I was here to catch him on it. If you ever need anything, you call me."

❧❧❧

That night after I got home, Dave showed up angrier than ever. He was yelling and pushing me into the wall — demanding to know what I'd said and who I'd told. His paranoia reached an all-time high, but I kept telling myself I only had to make it to the end of the quarter. Somehow I did.

Dave applied to the Coast Guard, and he was off to Basic Training. I went to work on my grandfather's ranch in Montana. It was the perfect chance to get away from him, to get away from it all and settle into a place where cell phone reception was impossible.

On the quiet Montana ranch, I breathed in the clean air and let the sun seep into my pores. I threw myself into working outside, but my thoughts still found me. Soon depression settled in. I was exhausted. I couldn't stop reliving every nightmare I'd endured. I felt dirty and damaged, and I didn't want to live anymore.

shattered

My grandfather called my mother and told her to come. He knew I needed her. Once she got there, I unleashed every secret I'd been holding in. I told her about Jason and Dave. I didn't leave anything out.

"I knew you were in trouble, Ashley, and I was concerned, but I also knew you were strong enough to get yourself out of whatever situation you were in. Have you had any contact with him since you left school?"

"I don't even know how he found the address, but he's been sending me letters. I haven't written back."

"Well, you need to respond. Be honest. Be strong. Tell him he's never going to touch you or see you again. Tell him to stay out of your life, and tell him you'll get a restraining order if he doesn't respect your wishes. Call him out on everything, Ashley. Lay it all out for him. Tell him what he's done and how he's made you feel. Tell him everything." I knew she was right.

I sat down and let my pain pour out onto paper. Even after all he'd done, I still didn't want to hurt Dave. I just wanted everything to be over. I wanted to be free. But Mom was right. I had to speak truth, even if it was the hardest thing I'd ever done — even if he didn't listen. It was time to stand up for myself.

Not long after I sent the letter, I found out Dave was discharged from the Coast Guard after receiving a psychological evaluation and deemed mentally unstable. Mixed emotions crowded in, and relief came with validation and understanding. I hadn't done anything wrong.

the will to fly

It wasn't me. He had a deep wound inside of him, and now he would get the help he needed.

❧ ❧ ❧

Dave was gone, and I could finally breathe free. I even had time to spend with family before going back to school. I needed to see my dad, and he wanted a rundown of college life.

"What happened with Dave?" That was all it took for me to break down in front of my father. I opened up to him, sharing with him all that I'd been through.

"Ashley, I had no idea." His concern and compassion soothed my broken soul. "I'm so sorry I wasn't there for you, but I know God was protecting you. Do you see that God was there? Ashley, you need to get back in church and pursue God. You need to know God. He loves you so much. He saved you through all of this. You know he was with you."

Dad was right, I knew, and I decided to go back to church. I wanted to let God in again. I was through hiding. I was ready to be found.

❧ ❧ ❧

I met Brad, and in comparison to all the darkness I'd been through, he seemed bright white. As far as relationships, I wanted to do things differently this time. We started out friends, and everything seemed wonderful at first. I'd decided not to sleep with anyone until I

shattered

married, but soon pressure came. The pressure triggered panic attacks, and Brad didn't know how to help me. He didn't understand the extent of the trauma and abuse I'd been through.

He wanted me to leave the past in the past and move forward with him. He couldn't understand, no matter how hard I tried to explain. Again, I found myself feeling disrespected, unwanted and unlovable. Nightmares about Dave began, and Brad felt betrayed by the dreams and memories.

I wanted the memories of Dave and all that he was to go away. I wanted to be rid of him. Why couldn't I keep him out of my thoughts?

I put pen to paper as lyrics swirled.

... Quit foolin' yourself, let's just forget about it
Don't clean up the past, just light a match and burn it
Erase me from your memory bank
It's time to move on, don't you think?
Too long I tortured myself over yesterday
You falsified who I was, used me in every wrong way
So I'm paintin' a new smile upon my face
Runnin' from the darkness, it's time for me to change

Cause that ain't what I asked for my life
To be used and abused and I'm embarrassed to say
That I was super-glued to the side of the Devil I couldn't recognize
But today I stand in the light and I'm saved by grace and I'll never
Remember that guy's face, cause I'm forever changed

the will to fly

By God's mercy and grace, my life is such a beautiful
place ...

... Like my superman he came into my world,
Gave me the key to the door,
When I walked through, the shackles round my ankles
broke and fell to the floor
I got no need for makeup, every day I wake up, I'm
more beautiful than before
Cause he don't own me anymore ...

༁༁༁

It was Easter. A friend from school and I decided to go
to a church in Seattle. As we made our way into the
sanctuary, I noticed tubs set up for a baptism service.
Initially, I wasn't interested. Worship music played, and
within moments, I knew. I sensed it was time to fully give
myself to God. I could feel how much he loved me.
Overwhelmed by my own love for him in return, I wanted
to take this next step.

The minister took a few minutes to talk about baptism
and what it meant. All who chose to come forward would
publicly identify with the death of Jesus Christ as they
were submerged in the water. As they rose up from the
water, they would be identifying with his resurrection, as it
reads in Colossians 2:12: "Having been buried with him in
baptism, in which you were also raised with him through
faith in the powerful working of God, who raised him
from the dead." I wanted everyone to know I belonged to

God. I wanted to publicly declare to God and the world that I was his.

Was I crazy? My family wasn't with me, and I knew my dad would be disappointed to miss this special time. But the feeling grew stronger, and I knew I needed to go. Every excuse fell away in comparison to what my heart wanted. I stood up from my seat and got in line.

All doubt dissipated, and I gave myself over to the process of following God. I wanted to be different, to change and to leave the past and all its misery behind.

I walked away from the church building that day, and only one truth floated through my insides: Today had been the best day of my life. I felt God's strength inside of me, and I knew anything was possible if I continued to follow him.

I called my dad to tell him the news, and he was so excited for me. He encouraged me to keep moving forward in my relationship with God. Then I called Brad. I was alive and full of hope and ready to share my news, but he wasn't happy. "I thought that was something we'd do together," he said, disappointed.

"It's not really something you do together, Brad. It's a personal decision. It was my declaration to make, and I knew the time was right."

After going ahead with my baptism, I optimistically moved to Idaho with Brad because he still outshined all my past relationships. Our dysfunction may have been different shades than what I shared with Jason and Dave, but I began to recognize the magnitude of our problems with every passing day. I grew more unhappy as every month flipped by on the calendar.

I couldn't be who I was meant to be or who God wanted me to be while we were living together. Here I was, hiding parts of my life from God again, and I knew what I needed to do, even though fears threatened me. If I left, where would I work and live? Would I always be alone? Ironically, I always found security and comfort in the uncomfortable situations of my life. As I sat in a brand-new mess, words flooded, and I rushed to pen the words to another song:

Way to You

I feel like someone sometimes
Fighting the will to fly
Hoping I can find a way to untwist the vines
For the fruit of trust to be filled up
Thoughts of doubt resigned

I want a way to you
Way to you
I want a way to you
A way to you

I feel like someone sometimes
Holding my thoughts inside
Keeps together peace, serenity
But my world divides
Afraid I'll burst out at the seams
I can't any longer hold my dreams

shattered

I can't decide
I am the fruit fed by the vine
And I create my world from the inside
So I'm letting go of my home
My life no longer my own ...

... You said it yourself and I confess
All blessings are of you
You give me my purpose
And so I decide no longer to deny
That my life is to be for you ...

... Now I feel like someone, sometimes
Spreading my wings to fly

కకక

As I bought my morning espresso that day at the drive-up window, God's voice became louder than ever. "Ashley, it's time to leave ... now!" So I went home, packed up and broke away from Brad and our three-year relationship. I knew it was time to go home, to rebuild who I was and to work on family relationships that had suffered. It was time to get back to my roots as a cowgirl and a singer and a daughter. For once, I was taking the time to concentrate on me and to discover who I was meant to be. I knew it was time for me to stop settling.

కకక

the will to fly

Our family had changed considerably over the past few years for the better. Both my parents were happily remarried, and we had all accepted our new normal. My stepmom and I even decided to attend a Christian conference together that featured Joyce Meyers. We walked in, took our seats in the huge auditorium and as soon as the music started, energy filled me with promise.

Every moment God seemed to show me how much he loved me. With every song the Jesus Culture band played, I sensed a deeper love growing inside me for God. I suddenly knew that my past experiences did nothing to diminish the ocean of love he wanted me to swim in.

With every message spoken, with every song sung, I could feel how big God's plans were for me. There were times I wanted to die — times I should have died — and yet he kept me alive for a specific purpose. I knew I wasn't a mistake. The truth burned in my heart. My life was valuable. God treasured me, and for the first time, I could believe the words echoing inside of me. *My life has worth.*

ॐॐॐ

There had been many ups and downs in my relationship with Brad, but I was forever grateful for one thing in particular. My time in Idaho had brought me to Christian Life Fellowship. One night during a music service, I asked God if he could use me. My past was now filled with things I never thought my story would hold, but I still wanted my life to count for more than the sum

shattered

of my experiences, both good and bad. My eyes closed, and a beautiful picture formed. I saw a group of teenagers singing with me as I led worship. It reminded me of my 14-year-old self who had brought her sad heart to a church in Montana and found it filled with peace. In that moment, my purpose was clear. Gratitude poured over me as I remembered the times of healing and growth I'd experienced that led me here.

Every detour, every scar, every dark moment I'd lived through had purpose. Pastor Doug and the people of Christian Life Fellowship watched me go from a girl with empty eyes to a girl glowing from the inside out. My friends said it was like watching a switch flip inside of me, and I could feel it. The depression was gone. The hopelessness was gone. I was happy, and life meant more than settling for less than what God had for me.

I didn't need to hide anymore. I let God find me, and he saw me as enough. I could finally hold my head high. I wasn't destined to be used and abused by others. I really had spread my wings to fly, and the view was more breathtaking than I ever imagined it would be.

a hand reaching out
The Story of Valerie
Written by Marty Minchin

My eyes narrowed with concentration as I held the little orange pill bottle under the trickle of gin. After my first taste of this magic liquid the night before, I couldn't think of anything cooler than sneaking a little to school. The pill bottle could easily be hidden in my book bag.

As the clear liquid filled the bottle, I savored the memory of the dry, bitter taste and the truly amazing feeling I'd gotten from my first drink.

My friend and I had spent the night before swigging gin from my parents' bar in the basement, and while she got a little sick, I got buzzed. All I wanted was to bring that feeling back.

A movement in the mirrored wall behind my bed caught my eye, and I fumbled to hide the bottle in my flowered cardboard nightstand.

"What's going on?" my mom asked, cocking her head at the gin bottle.

The bottle had tipped, and the liquid was running down the side of the furniture. I shoved my wet hands under my legs as I plopped on the bed.

It was time for quick thinking.

"What's that doing here?" I exclaimed, trying to match my mother's surprised expression. I stared at the bottle as if it had miraculously appeared in my room, trying to hide my terror.

"Hmmph."

The situation was undeniable. My parents' gin bottle was lying on my nightstand. My mom had just caught her 9-year-old daughter filling a pill bottle with liquor.

I lied, Mom yelled a little and that was that.

"It's time for school," she reminded me as she walked out of my room.

I stuffed the pill bottle in my school bag and followed her out.

I was never punished. My parents never brought up the incident again, giving me what I took as carte blanche to become a child alcoholic right under their noses.

కకక

My childhood, at least on the surface, was not one that would typically lend itself to early drinking. My parents had settled in a small town in the Treasure Valley where they raised my brother and me. My mom had a job in media publications, and my dad worked for the city. They worked hard to advance in their careers, and they were responsible and good with money. My brother and I walked or rode our bikes to school, and we spent many afternoons playing outside or hanging out at friends' houses.

Our middle-class exterior, however, hid an unhappier world that ate at my soul. My dad was a typical 1960s-era

a hand reaching out

father who worked hard, provided well and never showed affection. "I love you" was not in his vocabulary. My mom and I had a strangely inverted relationship, where she treated me more like a close friend than a young daughter. She shared details of her life that were too mature for my ears, and she sought my advice when I was too young to even know what she was talking about. Other times, she'd yell and scream at me, calling me "stupid" and telling me I made no sense. When I cried after my grandmother's beloved German shepherd died, my mom told me to shut up because I was being dumb. I was convinced that she didn't care about me. She couldn't even bring herself to issue a punishment when she caught me with the liquor bottle in fourth grade.

After my first buzz, my secret trips downstairs to raid my parents' liquor cabinet became regular outings. Depression set in early in my life, and alcohol was the perfect antidote. I usually chose gin or vodka, which I could refill with water. My parents, who were extremely responsible drinkers, never once remarked that their alcohol seemed weak.

For the most part, I hid my new habit. I preferred to drink alone, as alcohol was shocking to most of my elementary-school peers. I'd break out the bottle only with a select few who I trusted would not rat to their parents. As I got older and formed groups of friends, a circle of troublemakers began to orbit around me. Often, I was the one who instigated the bad behavior. I figured out that if we sat quietly outside the fence around my yard, we could pick up the lit cigarette butts my dad threw over and finish smoking them.

Not all of my friends were rebels in training. I was a nice kid, a pleaser, and when I wasn't down on myself, I enjoyed spending time with kids who I secretly believed were too good for me. In sixth grade, Lisa — who was born on the same day as me — was one of my three "good" friends who believed in God and was always inviting me to Christian events. Usually I was too busy smoking and drinking with my other friends, but one night I did accept an invitation to spend the night at Lisa's house.

After attending a church service, we headed straight into her "play closet," a large walk-in closet that her parents had converted into a playroom. She began talking about being "saved."

"Saved?" I asked. "What's saved?"

Lisa was saying something about God, who was not a stranger to me. My parents weren't religious, but they faithfully put my brother and me on the Sunday school bus that came around every week to ferry neighborhood kids to church. We attended church occasionally as a family.

Most of the knowledge I had about God came from my grandmother, who had a fiery love for God and the Bible. She loved to read to me from the book of Revelation, which describes the end of the world. I loved to listen, and her exclamations of, "The beast is a'coming! The beast is a'coming soon!" were deliciously scary.

a hand reaching out

To answer my question, Lisa pulled out her Bible and flipped through the thin pages until she found the section she was looking for. She began to read.

The words didn't make much sense to me, but they sounded beautiful. Whatever she was reading about, I wanted. I needed it.

"Do you want to talk to God?" Lisa asked, looking up from the book. "Do you want to tell him you're sorry for the things you've done wrong and start a friendship with him?"

"Yeah, I think I want that."

Together, we bowed our heads as we sat side-by-side on the play closet floor. Lisa would say a line of the prayer, and I'd repeat her words.

A sense of peace settled over me like a warm blanket. I knew I had done the right thing. But I didn't know how to change my life.

When I walked out of Lisa's house the next morning, I stepped onto the same wandering path I'd been traveling. I tried hard to be a better person and do the right thing, but it never worked out. The sidewalks of my path would still be littered with liquor bottles and cigarette butts as I searched for a way to drown the self-loathing that was growing in me like a cancer. But somewhere deep inside, God was with me. I just wasn't ready to fully acknowledge him yet.

❧ ❧ ❧

shattered

The small-town atmosphere where we lived, where everyone knew everyone and bad stuff rarely happened, lulled my parents into believing that allowing my brother and me to run freely around the neighborhood — and later around town — was a good idea. Parties were easy to find, and my parents never asked where I was or when I'd be home. I was now old enough to babysit, and I passed on my earnings to my brother's friends, who were happy to buy me alcohol. If my babysitting money ran out, I'd sneak a $20 bill from my mom's purse to keep my liquor supply flush.

At home, my inner battles raged, and the contents of the growing collection of empty liquor bottles decorating my headboard couldn't make the dark pit inside me go away. I hid bottles of Jack Daniels, vodka, Mad Dog 20/20 and 7-Up in my big walk-in closet, and I shamelessly added the empties to my public display. When my mom asked me where the bottles came from, I told her that I'd found them. The bottles were an invitation for her to probe deeper into my inner turmoil, but she never questioned my story.

I deeply wanted someone — anyone — to care about me.

My brother, who was three years older, was not a candidate. When we'd stand together at the bus stop, other kids would push me into pokey evergreens covered with cobwebs. They called me names and laughed at me, and he stood by silently. When I went to his room to talk, he'd tell me to get out and leave me alone.

a hand reaching out

Mom was equally unmoving, but hardly anyone knew it. Outside of our house, people thought she was the sweetest, nicest person they had ever met. She smiled in town, but screamed and yelled at me at home. She took everything I said the wrong way, and when I tried to talk to her about something important, she nodded and "uh-huh-ed," rarely even responding with a full sentence.

I was eaten up with worry when doctors found a lump in her breast that needed to be removed and tested. Despite her gruff treatment of me, I always treated her with respect and never talked back. While she was at her biopsy, I wrote her a note and told her how much I loved her. At the bottom, I signed my name and drew a smiley face with two great big round eyes and an oblong nose below it.

She sank into the couch when she got home, and I handed her the note. I stepped back to watch her read it, hoping my words might brighten her up a little. When she looked up at me, her eyes were brimming with anger.

"I know what this is!" she screamed.

I stepped back in surprise.

"Mom, what are you talking about?"

She waved the paper in the air and pointed at the smiley face's nose.

"Those are boobs!" She threw the paper on the floor in disgust. "You're making fun of me!"

I could never do anything right. I slunk out of the living room, up the stairs and into my closet, where a bottle of vodka was waiting.

shattered

৯৯৯

When I looked into the small mirror in my bathroom, I cried. The mirror had three panels, and I could arrange them so that I could see my awful self at all angles.

The girl who looked back at me had fair skin and too-thick blond hair, an inheritance from my father.

I hated her. I screamed horrible names at her. I banged my head against the wall and punched myself in the face. I lifted up my heavy, course hair, grabbed chunks the width of dimes and yanked them out. If there was any pain, I gladly absorbed it.

Long before the Emo movement made cutting a popular way to self-inflict pain, I had figured out how to slice my hands right behind the knuckles. I'd cut as deeply as I could and then wind gauze around my wounds. When someone asked, I told him or her I'd burnt my hands on the woodstove in our basement.

My hair pulling turned out to be a popular party trick. No one believed I'd do it, and then they'd gape as I ripped a handful out by the roots. Often, it felt good because I felt like I was getting the punishment I deserved for being such an unlikeable person. It felt right to me when someone treated me meanly or yelled at me. That's why most of my friends were unsavory — their company was more comfortable than that of nice people.

I got a job at Taco Time when I was 14, and the steady income bought me more freedom — and more alcohol. During the week, I drank enough before and after school and between classes to feed my buzz. My partying intensified on the weekends, when I drank to get completely wasted.

My friends and I had figured out how to make bongs out of pop cans, so we often smoked marijuana, too. Older kids down the street regularly threw parties when their parents went out of town, and a dollar at the door was the only fee for a night of alcoholic bliss. No one cared how old you were or who you came with.

In 1984, when I was 15, my family went elk hunting and stayed in a cabin in the wilderness. My friend Alana was spending the weekend with us, and we immediately sniffed out a nearby house full of teenage boys. When I asked my parents if we could hang out with these strangers, they replied, "Sure."

I wasn't expecting such an easy yes. My dad was a reformed bad boy from the 1950s, when "bad" meant smoking, driving fast and making out with girls. My mom was a good girl from Payette, Idaho, and she had turned my dad into an upstanding community man. They assumed their children were equally upstanding and were always doing the right thing. To me, it looked like they didn't care.

Not ones to miss a party, Alana and I headed out the cabin door as quickly as our parents gave us their naïve consent. When we walked into the neighboring cabin, the familiar sight of teenagers sitting around drinking greeted us. We knew we were in the right place. After a few hours, we checked back in at my parents' cabin to uphold our

shattered

façade of virtue, and then we snuck out after they went to bed.

The second time I opened the door, I looked up to see an average-looking guy walking down the stairs. Something happened. It wasn't love at first sight, but something inside me told me to pay attention to this guy.

I had indulged in a few drinks on my first trip to the house, but I was so interested in Trip that for the first time in years I didn't pick up a glass.

At rare times in my life, I had found myself in fleeting sweet spots that usually only materialized when I was drunk or high. As I sank into the couch next to Trip and our conversation stretched until 2 a.m., I was so engrossed that I didn't feel the urge to drink or smoke. For a few hours, I reveled in the sweet conversation with someone significant.

Trip walked us back to our cabin, and we parted ways without any plans to see each other again. He was born and raised in the same town as me, but he was a shy guy who had dated around but had never had a serious relationship. His mother had been murdered when he was a little boy, and he was quiet and withdrawn. His friends hounded him to call me for two weeks. I was thrilled when he finally called to ask me out on a date, but I had to broach the subject of our age difference with my parents first.

"Mom," I ventured, "this guy asked me out."

In her typical fashion, she didn't ask for details.

"I just want you to meet him and see what you think."

a hand reaching out

"Just go out with him. It's fine."

I fidgeted as I laid out the potential problem with Trip.

"There's just one thing."

"Valerie, what one thing?"

Here came the bombshell.

"He's 18."

The potential explosive fizzled. "What's the problem? I've let you go out with your brother's friends."

I was 15 and had just started my sophomore year of high school. Trip was 18, a high school graduate and living on his own.

"He's out of school, and he's actually almost 19."

Still no resistance. My dad turned around to chime in. "We'll meet him."

Wonderstruck at how well the conversation went, I accepted Trip's invitation. My parents did a little due diligence. Through my father's connections in the community, he asked around about Trip and his dad. My mom talked to my brother about him. There wasn't much to uncover. Trip was a good kid, not big on partying or drinking. We were green-lighted for a date at the movies.

Trip was sweet and gentlemanly. He borrowed a '57 Chevy for our dates. Unlike many guys in the 1980s, he didn't spend the date trying to make out with me. When our dates turned into a relationship, we both knew that we weren't going to date anyone else. For a 19 year old and a 15 year old, our relationship was surprisingly mature — in some ways.

In other ways, however, little changed. I still drank,

and now I had a boyfriend to buy my alcohol. He never questioned what I wanted, even when I had him buy two-liter bottles of California Cooler that I could drink in a sitting. While he was reticent, drinking turned me into the life of the party.

Trip and I weren't clingy or dramatic, even when, after a year of dating, he moved to Portland with his construction job. He came home every weekend to see me, and I never cheated on him in between. He picked me up every Friday night at whatever party I was attending and drove me home so I wouldn't drive drunk.

But when Trip started getting serious about our relationship, I balked. I was still in high school, and he was a working man staring at the rest of his life. Plus, for the first time, another guy had caught my eye.

Eric, a Mormon boy at my school, was appealing enough for me to break it off with Trip. Eric and I started dating during my junior year, and I quickly was drawn into his close-knit family who had strong religious values. Contrasted with my depression and miserable family life, Eric's wonderful family was a welcome alternative.

My drinking and smoking proved to be indirectly proportional to my happiness. The more I was drawn to Eric, his family and his church, the less I partied.

I began attending church with Eric and going through training sessions with the Mormon missionaries, even though negative comments my parents had made about Mormonism prickled in my mind. The people seemed so nice and so good. How could this be wrong?

a hand reaching out

I did wonder sometimes, though. When I read the Bible, some of the verses didn't jibe with what I was learning in the Mormon church. My doubt was put to the test when the church asked me to set a date to be baptized.

My lukewarm parents were jarred into action when I told them I was considering becoming a Mormon. Eric came to my house to talk with my parents about it one night, and my dad threw out an ultimatum.

"If you leave with him, you don't come back," he said, crossing his arms over his chest.

I walked out the door with Eric and went to his house.

"It's okay," Eric's mother assured me. "Heavenly Father loves you, and you have a new family now."

My parents weren't ready to let me go that easily, though, and within hours, my mom was knocking on the door. She told me Dad was ready to talk, and I could come home now.

"Why on earth would I go back?" Did my mom think she could offer me something better? She stood her ground, waiting.

Eric broke the stalemate.

"You need to go home and reconcile with your family." His gentle voice made sense.

I found my dad sitting on his bed upstairs. His head was down.

"Hi, Dad."

He didn't respond, so I made the peace offering.

"I love you, Dad."

The silence hung in the air for an eternity as I waited

for the words I had never heard my dad say. Maybe the thought of losing me finally drug them out of him.

"I love you, too, Valerie."

I stayed home that night.

❧❧❧

The next day, I went back to Eric's house, but visiting Mormon missionaries sent me home to talk to God about whether I should be baptized. I pulled out the new Bible my grandmother had given me for a graduation gift, but before I could open it, my friend Stacy called.

Stacy loved God, and she urged me not to become a Mormon, reminding me that Mormon teachings did not line up with the Bible. For example, she said, the Mormons believe that men can become gods. A twinge inside me affirmed her words. I couldn't identify exactly what it was, but I sensed that God did not want me to be baptized in Eric's church. I told the missionaries I needed more time to think.

What I really needed was more time to read the Bible. When Eric went away to college, I had more free time. The more I read and learned about God, the hungrier I became to know God more. I'd stay awake until 2 or 3 a.m., reading the Bible and highlighting verses that stuck out to me with different colored highlighters. The words came alive, and even though I was reading the outdated language of the King James version, every sentence made sense. I highlighted Philippians 4:7: "And the peace of

a hand reaching out

God, which passeth all understanding, shall keep your hearts and minds through Christ Jesus." *Can this really happen?* I wondered. *Is this really true?* Yes, I believed it could.

The verses Matthew 11:28-30 also caught my attention. "Come unto me, all ye that labour and are heavy laden, and I will give you rest. Take my yoke upon you, and learn of me; for I am meek and lowly in heart: and ye shall find rest unto your souls. For my yoke is easy, and my burden is light."

That's awesome! God is going to give me peace, and it won't involve drinking. He is going to give me rest.

Reading the Bible transformed me from the inside. I felt and thought differently. I began to feel better about myself. I knew I wasn't perfect, and some bad things had happened, but I no longer screamed obscenities at my image in the mirror. My drinking tapered off to the point where I was only having the occasional glass.

My feelings for Eric also began to dissipate. When he came home from college, I didn't want him around. He left for two years of missionary service, and the more he was gone, the more I read the Bible. I hardly considered him when I took a job as a nanny in Philadelphia, where I lived with the family that hired me. With time alone and no boyfriend around, my relationship with God continued to deepen.

As my connection with Eric faded, Trip found his way back into my life. He had never disappeared completely; the first time I ever saw him drunk was when we broke up, and he continued to stop by my house in the year afterward. I'd sometimes see him parked outside my house, and there were awkward situations where he and Eric were both seated in my parents' living room. When Eric moved away, Trip restarted his weekend visits home from Portland. When I moved to Pennsylvania, Trip began to call. I talked to God about our renewed relationship, and I sensed that Trip — even though he was not following God — was the man I was supposed to marry. When Trip flew to Philadelphia to ask me to be his wife, I accepted. I knew it was the right thing to do.

When I moved back home after my year on the East Coast, my mom encouraged me to move in with Trip. I had lost my virginity to him when I was 15, but I wouldn't do it. My nervousness was more complex than the question of whether to live with Trip. I decided to get my own apartment.

"I don't know how you can marry Trip," a friend told me one night. She had grown up with emotional abuse, and we connected over our shared childhood experiences.

"He's too nice."

I nodded in agreement. We talked about how we liked when people were mean to us because we didn't know what to do when people were nice. Trip was loving and caring, and he really listened to me.

As my friend's words sank in, my confidence in my relationship got caught in my inner whirlpool of doubt. *Maybe he is too good for me. Maybe I don't deserve to be with someone like him.*

a hand reaching out

For the first time in more than a year, I poured myself a glass of liquor. My friend Jerry, an old buddy from my party days, stopped by my place to visit, and I left him in the living room while I went to the bathroom for an aspirin. I'd hurt my toe a while before, and it was aching.

As I rummaged through the cupboard, I remembered a recorded tape Eric had sent me. We hadn't talked in a long time — not since I'd sent him a "Dear John" letter in which I'd cleverly written "Dear John" before lightly erasing the "John" and writing "Eric" over it. I stuck the tape in a cassette player and listened to Eric's voice telling me he loved me. *Was I doing the right thing?* I wasn't sure anymore.

I let the Tylenol 3 pills pour into my palm as I looked in the mirror. The ugly girl stared back — the one who hated herself and pulled out her own hair. I watched myself in the mirror guzzle the pills as those old feelings flooded over me.

Jerry found me on the floor of the bathroom. I mumbled what I had done, and he called my mom and drove me to the ER.

"This needs to be reported because it was a suicide attempt," the ER doctor told my mom. She begged him to let me go home with her as I spouted out a fountain of information about my turbulent relationship with my mom.

"Look," my mom said calmly, trying to negate the history of abuse I'd told the doctor. "I promise I'll take care of her. We'll get family counseling. She'll get better."

shattered

I smiled with relief.

Thank you, Lord Jesus. Finally, my mom and I are going to reconcile. She does love me. Thank you, God.

We got back to my parents' house around 3 a.m., and I collapsed on the couch. Mom trudged upstairs without another word.

A few hours later, I heard her moving about as she got dressed and left for work. Her office was close to the house, and she frequently stopped by home to use the bathroom or check in. By midday, I had already called my boss and said I wasn't coming in. I needed to rest.

"Aren't you going to get up and go to work?" Mom's sharp words woke me from my midday nap.

"Um, not today. I need a little time."

So much for a new start to our relationship. "Are you kidding?" Her voice had already escalated into a yell. "I was up all night with you, and I'm at work! You're not even going to try?"

I barely contained my sobs until she slammed the door on her way out. When the tears finally subsided, my choices became clear. I could kill myself for real, or I could get myself together and do what I knew was right. My mom was never going to be there for me the way I wanted. I had myself, and I had God. She wasn't going to change, so it was up to me to deal with it.

My life changed so quickly in that moment that it felt like God had reached down, grabbed me by the collar and yanked me out of a situation I'd wallowed in for almost two decades. It was time to change.

a hand reaching out

The first order of business was to call Trip. I told him what had happened and apologized. It was time to get excited about my wedding. I left drinking and my broken relationship with my mom in the past. God and Trip were my future.

≈≈≈

God began to talk to me about my relationship with my mom. I began to see her as a precious little egg that you have to hold carefully. She needed a little extra care, and I realized that I might never have the close relationship with her that I ached for.

God showed me how to set healthy boundaries — and even stand up to her.

I walked in on my mom trying on her dress for my wedding, days before the big event, and I was shocked when I saw her ribs protruding from her back. She was disturbingly thin, bordering on anorexic.

I was rude to her.

"Mom." She looked up at me. "You look disgusting."

I meant only love, but the words tumbled out harshly. She and my dad were having troubles, and I could see where this was leading. Anorexia was prevalent — not long before, Karen Carpenter's death from the disease had been all over the news. My heart pounded as I waited for Mom's reaction.

She took a step toward me, raised her arm and slapped me across the face.

shattered

"I'm sorry, Mom, but I love you. You look terrible. You're way too thin."

Then I walked out the bedroom door.

A few days later, Mom apologized. The slap had arisen from shock, and she admitted that she was anorexic. Even though I had been rude, Mom realized that I loved her enough to be honest.

❧❧❧

Trip and I got married in 1989 and soon joined a local church. I took a job at the church, and soon the pastor and his wife became close friends. I poured my heart out to them, and they became like surrogate parents and grandparents to me and my growing family.

Trip wasn't as devoted to God when we joined the church. He preferred to hang out with his construction crew, and he drank a lot after work. When our daughter was born, however, he stopped drinking and started driving the Sunday school bus. Soon he joined me in working with the church's teenagers, and we were both baptized.

A few years later, we found our way to Christian Life Fellowship and got plugged in. If there was a Bible study on marriage, we were there. Trip joined a church men's group. He listened to Christian music radio stations when he drove the backhoe. After almost a decade of marriage, we had three kids, a healthy life at our church and strong relationships with God.

a hand reaching out

My devotion to Bible reading taught me that even if I didn't know how to handle a situation, I could read the Bible and talk to God, and God would tell me what to do. Trip still worked out of town a lot, and early in our marriage, God had showed me that I needed to surprise him on a regular basis when he was away on a job. I frequently packed up the kids and drove to his job sites, only staying home if the drive was too far for the little ones.

After a particularly moving church service at Christian Life Fellowship, Trip pulled me aside.

"God told me that I needed to tell you something tonight." His intensity took me aback. Did he have cancer? Did he get drunk a few times? Was he on drugs?

"Valerie, are you ready to hear this?" His voice stuttered, and he looked down at the floor. "You need to sit down."

I slowly backed into the church seat.

"While I was in a little town in Idaho six years ago, I came this close …" He held his hand in the air, pinching his thumb and index finger together to show me how close. "I almost cheated on you."

The devastation was instantaneous. I jumped up and pushed past Trip on my way to the women's bathroom, where I broke down in sobs in front of the mirror. A friend trailed behind me, crying and praying with me. When I composed myself enough to come out, Trip was waiting outside the door with his arms open.

"Valerie, I don't want this to get between us." He

engulfed me in a huge hug, squeezing me to his chest. "I don't want to hurt our marriage. I'm going to do whatever it takes to get through this."

It's all going to be okay. I felt God's presence as he spoke words into my mind. *It's going to be better than it ever was before.*

My cries finally subsided into sniffles, and we walked together into the parking lot. His words of assurance rang in my ears, little flickers of hope that we could handle this.

૭૪૭૪૭૪

I holed up in my house to deal with the emotions creeping in. We told no one. When my neighbors stopped by and gently asked how we were, I replied, "Just pray." I didn't ask Trip for details, but that didn't stop my mind from conjuring them up.

When Trip hugged me, I wondered if he'd held her like that. When he kissed me, I wondered if he kissed her the same way. Despite Trip's promises outside the church bathroom, the thought of his infidelity was getting between us.

Several weeks later, I spilled the story to Pastor Doug at Christian Life Fellowship.

"I wish you would have come to me the day after," he said. "The first few days are so important." He met with Trip and me for counseling, and we started talking about our relationship.

"I don't know," I admitted. "I love him, and he made a

mistake." My heart, though, didn't entirely match my words. I was angry and hurt.

Our pastor gave Trip homework, small things he could do to work things through with me. But when we got home from our sessions, he would never do them. Week after week, Trip had nothing to report to our pastor at our meetings. Pastor Doug finally told him there was no point in us coming back. Until Trip put effort into fixing our marriage, nothing would change.

"What do I do?" I asked our pastor at church one day.

"Let me try talking to Trip alone," he suggested. "Maybe we can make some progress that way."

Trip went a few times. He and Pastor Doug talked about how his mother was murdered, and Trip said that he had learned that in life you don't need other people when you can do things yourself.

When the counseling sessions stopped, Trip's relationship with God noticeably went downhill. He didn't seem to want to go to church. He would occasionally attend the men's group and participate in various ministries, but when I took a job working with the church's children, he became annoyed.

"Why do you have to do that?" he'd ask in a disgusted voice as I headed out to work. Not long before, he would have driven to church with me to help.

"What if Trip never changes?" Pastor Doug asked one day, sensing my despair.

Once again, God reached down and handed me a clear choice.

shattered

I could not change my husband. No amount of dragging him to classes, forcing him to listen to Bible teaching or asking him to read helpful books would guarantee a difference. I needed to work on myself and figure out how I could love and honor my husband — even if he never changed — for the rest of my life.

࿏࿏࿏

Even though I worked hard to change myself, there were days when I wallowed in pity parties and struggled to forgive Trip. Helping other people, I slowly was learning, was the antidote.

I glanced around the chapel one summer day as the children from three different churches, who had gathered there for church camp, listened to a talk about forgiveness. As the camp director, it was my job to take care of these kids and help them when needed.

At the end of the session, the speaker asked the children to come to the front of the church if they wanted to talk or pray about anything. I noticed a little girl sitting on the floor off to the side. She was slumped over and pressing her face into her hands. Her dirty blond hair hid her face.

"Are you okay?" I sat down next to the tiny girl, hoping she'd talk to me.

She looked up. Tears ran down her face.

"There's someone in my life I haven't forgiven," she said.

a hand reaching out

As she described the feelings in her heart, I struggled to hold back my own tears. Her words mirrored my own struggle to forgive Trip, even though her issues were with a brother with a bad attitude.

God spoke to me. *Listen to what you are saying to this little girl. Then tell yourself the same thing.*

I heard him. It was time to take my own advice. As I prayed with the little girl, I asked God to change her heart so that she could truly forgive her brother. I prayed silently that I could forgive Trip.

"Now, let's pray for your brother," I suggested. "What's his name?"

"Trip."

I sat straight up. What were the chances of her brother and my husband having the same name?

Unable to stop my tears, I helped her talk to God.

"Repeat after me," I told her gently, "just as if you were talking to your brother if he was sitting with us." My words for her became words for my own heart.

"Trip, you have done some things that hurt my feelings."

"Trip, I forgive you."

"Trip, I love you."

I hugged her close. I thought my role was to help her. But God was using my work with children to heal *me*.

I recounted the story to one of our pastors later. "I thought this was about the kids, not about me."

He laughed. "God often works through us while we serve others."

shattered

My role helping others at the church suddenly became clear. God had multiple plans for me as I served people at the church. One of them was my own healing.

❦ ❦ ❦

Eventually, Trip told me some details about his encounter with the other woman. He was working far from home that week, and he had gone to a bar with friends. He met a lady there, and they got in the car together to go back to her house. He never went inside, but he came close to sleeping with her in the car. I stopped the story there. Pastor Doug and Pastor Julie warned me that too many details could be harmful.

As time passed, Trip became angry and bitter. I knew that he had never forgiven the man who had killed his mom, and decades of unforgiveness festered inside him. He didn't seem interested in God anymore, and in his pain, he began lashing out at me.

The names I'd once screamed at myself in the mirror now poured out of Trip's mouth. At times, he sounded just like my mother, telling me I was useless and couldn't do anything right. When our youngest daughter was in middle school, she began suffering from the turmoil in our home. I talked to God with her, and then I decided to write a letter to Trip. I needed to stop being so nice and tell him how much he was hurting our family. I needed to stop being the victim and lovingly stand up to my husband.

a hand reaching out

I poured out my heart in the letter, but I put my pen down before I finished the fourth page. I had written words of love, words of sadness and words of pain. I assured Trip I didn't want to leave him and would do anything to help him. *Maybe this letter needs something else,* I thought.

I went back to see Pastor Doug and showed him the letter. He approved of the way I had openly shared how I felt. "However," he said, "I think you need to end it with an ultimatum." I knew he was right.

I took a deep breath and wrote the words. I couldn't keep my daughter and myself in this situation any longer. If he didn't improve his behavior, we'd have to leave.

When he came home from work, I handed him the folded pages. He read them, but the change wasn't what I'd hoped for.

Trip still doesn't attend church that often. He has very bad days. His anger is unpredictable, and while the emotional abuse has stopped, he can still be mean.

The crazy thing is, I love him deeply, anyway.

స్రా స్రా స్రా

I have learned that healing is not about waiting for the person who has hurt you to change. It's not about what that person does or says. It's about *me* doing what God wants me to and that is to love them unconditionally. As I've grown to know God more, he has healed *me*. He even used my efforts to serve others as a path to be healed

shattered

myself. God has given *me* a wild love for my husband that I could never muster on my own. God has also helped me create healthy boundaries so that I can keep away from potential hurtful situations with Trip. No matter what my husband throws at me, God has helped me respond with love, playfulness and affection. And it's working.

He can still fly into a rage over the tiniest offense. Recently, he huffed in muttering about someone who'd upset him.

As he worked himself up to a rant, I gave him a look and shook my head a little. Several years ago, I would have broken down crying, and Trip would have yelled at me for that, too. Today, I strode over and gave him a giant smooch.

He smiled. I know this instant good mood won't last, but for now, I'll take it.

going the distance
The Story of Ben and Katie
Written by Karen Koczwara

An angry boy with a black eye, searching for purpose,
something bigger than himself.
A spunky, athletic girl with a hurting heart and a reason to run.
A lonely, young Marine in combat boots,
treading the dusty Middle Eastern terrain.
A girl desperate for answers and a fresh start.
Twelve hundred miles separate their worlds.
Boy meets girl, and two hearts collide.
But can their love survive the distance?
Or will their differences tear them apart?

༺ ༺ ༺

I was born in Yakima, Washington, in 1983. My parents moved us to Tumwater, a small city outside Olympia, when I was young. In many ways, my childhood was idyllic. My parents demonstrated a deep love for one another and passed their affection on to me. We regularly visited the local Catholic church, and my parents often talked about their faith in God. But despite my happy home, a subtle anger stirred in me.

I attended a private Catholic school, and in third grade, I began picking fights with the other kids. I could not put my finger on what troubled me so much. Many of my peers came from broken homes, and I knew I had it good. What was at the root of my angst?

After too many scuffles on the playground, the school principal stepped in to intervene. "You need to take this kid to anger management classes, or he won't be able to stay at the school," he informed my parents.

His words greatly upset me, as I did not want to leave the school. I wanted to be a good kid, but I had difficulty controlling myself. If someone said something that upset me, my body shook from the inside out, and I felt as if fire might spew from my nostrils at any moment. My parents took me to a counselor, who tried to give me helpful techniques to tame my temper. But his efforts seemed futile. I decided that I'd just be a bit craftier about my ways and try to avoid picking fights. This worked for a while, but my insides still roared with anger and frustration.

In high school, I switched to a public school and discovered I was years ahead of my peers academically. My private school education had given me an edge. I threw myself into sports and prided myself on my athletic ability. I gave up on the Catholic faith, no longer interested in attending church or discussing spiritual things. *I believe there is a God,* I told myself. *But I don't really want anything to do with him right now.*

My anger still plagued me. Occasionally, I initiated a scuffle with other guys at school. During my junior year, a teacher approached me with a piercing question.

"What are you afraid of?" she asked pointedly.

After pondering the question for a while, I finally came

to a conclusion. I was afraid of living a meaningless life. *I don't want to waste any opportunity,* I realized. *When my funeral rolls around, I want people to remember me. I want to rack up as many achievements as possible so that life doesn't pass me by. I don't want to be a nobody.*

The acknowledgment was profound. *Does this explain why I'm so angry all the time?*

After graduation, I attended college, but I hated every minute of it. *This is boring,* I thought, restless for something more adventurous. Instead, I decided to join the Marines. My father had been a Marine, and he spoke highly of the military branch. *Maybe that is what I'm meant to do,* I decided. *Joining the Marines will help me find something bigger out there, something purposeful.*

I walked into the recruiter's office in April 2003. "I'd like to join the Marines," I announced.

The recruiters joked that I was a dream candidate. I easily passed the exam and had no special requests or health problems. "You're going to do just great," they assured me.

I went through boot camp and then attended A-school, where I studied to be an avionics electrician. The training was intensive, but I succeeded at it. In February 2004, I returned to Florida after leave for more schooling during training. One day, I participated in a series of "fireman carries," which entailed lifting another person on my back. At 5 feet, 11 inches and 175 pounds, I was of average stature. After running sprints with another guy on my back, I felt a searing pain shoot up the left side of my

shattered

stomach. A doctor exam shortly after revealed a substantial hernia from lifting too much weight.

"It looks like we're going to have to operate to repair your stomach wall," the doctor informed me.

The surgery left me bedridden for three weeks. I grew restless and anxious, thrashing in my bed as the minutes slowly ticked by on the clock. Having always been an active guy, I had a very difficult time sitting still. Loneliness and depression soon kicked in. My parents, still living on the West Coast, were unable to fly out to see me, and the days grew long and dull. *I've gotta get out of here,* I thought in a panic, my mind racing as I stared out the hospital window. *This totally sucks.*

One especially agonizing night, I decided to pray. I hadn't talked to God much in years, but I hoped he might still hear my feeble, desperate cry. "God, if you can get me out of this place where I am so angry and alone, I will serve you. I just can't go on like this anymore."

A short time later, I was completely healed and able to return to work. Gratitude overwhelmed me. God had heard my prayers after all! I was going to be okay.

I went on to C-school in California for more extensive training that summer. There, I met a great group of guys who became like brothers. We received orders to Yuma, Arizona, in August. With its barren, dusty terrain, Yuma was a far cry from the lush green coastal mountains of my home state. I acclimated soon enough, however, grateful to be reunited with my buddies. One of my friends seemed especially different since arriving at our new base. When I asked him what the deal was, he eagerly responded.

"I found a great church, man. You should check it out with me sometime."

Church. Hmph. I hadn't set foot in a church in years. The idea didn't particularly excite me, but I was intrigued by my friend's sudden change in demeanor. I reluctantly agreed to give it a try.

After my first visit to the church, I was not especially impressed. The preacher reminded me a lot of myself — a bit loud and aggressive. I decided I didn't much care for him or for church in general. I returned to my partying ways, drinking and exchanging callous banter with the guys. My friend, however, remained persistent.

"No pressure, man, but if you ever want to go to Bible study with me, I'd love to see you there," he said.

I appreciated my friend's genuine concern. "I'll check it out," I told him.

Something shifted inside me as I sat in that Bible study a few days later. I slowly put my guard down as I listened to the other guys talk about God and read from their Bibles. I'd always assumed religious stuff was for sissies, but seeing these tough Marines praying touched me deeply. *Maybe you can still be tough and cool and have faith in God,* I concluded.

The guys talked about God's love and how he wanted a relationship with us. They discussed the hope, peace and joy one could experience by giving his or her life over to God. The setting was much more intimate than the ritualistic services I'd attended at the Catholic church. I leaned in, hanging on every word. *I want that hope, peace and joy. I'm tired of being this angry guy all the time, always searching for meaning. Is this what I've been looking for all along?*

At the end of the study, the leader asked if anyone would like to invite God into his life. "If you are ready to accept him right now, please just raise your hand," he said. "He is waiting to begin a relationship with you that will last for eternity."

Immediately, my hand shot up. I still had many questions about God and the Bible, but I knew enough to know that this was what I wanted. I'd spent my whole life searching for something bigger than myself, and now I knew what that was. God was that missing piece, the only one who could fill the void in my heart and heal my wounds. Only he offered true purpose. I was ready to begin a life with him.

That fall, discussion about deployment to Iraq began to circulate at my base.

"Does anyone want to volunteer to go before we pick names?" our leaders asked.

I stopped to consider the idea. There was no reason not to volunteer. "I'll go," I spoke up.

In November, I deployed to Iraq for six months. One of my new friends, who also had invited God into his life, signed up to deploy with me, also.

"I want to help you, Ben," he told me. "You are going to Iraq for the first time, and you're a new Christian. I hope we can encourage each other while we're there."

going the distance

Living in Yuma had prepared me for the terrain and weather I'd experience overseas. Iraq, as expected, was dry, dusty and very hot. Because I was still of lower rank, I spent much of my time on watch duties, patrolling our large air base there. I occasionally worked on the aircrafts, too, putting my new skills to use. Once a week, the enemy indirectly fired at us, but for the most part, my time there was peaceful and smooth, and I never felt unsafe.

During my deployment, I grew to understand and love God more deeply. I read my Bible daily, eager to see what God had to say to me. The stories inside the pages leapt to life as I pored over them. My friend continued to encourage me, reminding me that God could take even the most discouraging things in our life and use them for good. I recalled my surgery and how I'd spent weeks thrashing anxiously in that bed as I recovered. I'd felt so helpless at the time, but God had healed me, and now that I knew him, I could see that he'd been with me all along. He had known my journey would bring me all the way overseas, where I'd learn to trust him and rely on him in new ways. I was excited to see what he had in store when I returned.

I flew back to the United States in April 2005, more excited about God than ever. With my friend's help, I now understood that being a Christian did not mean giving up my macho military ways. I could still be manly and love God at the same time. I hoped more guys in my unit would discover this, too.

Shortly after returning to Yuma, I decided to attend

something called Encounter at my new church. The church put this three-day event on a few times a year. It was a time for both those who had just invited God into their lives and those who had known him for some time to draw closer to him. I'd heard great things about it, and I was eager to check it out.

As expected, the Encounter was an amazing, healing and emotional time. We sang songs to God, spent time in prayer and broke up into groups where we openly shared what God had shown us during the weekend. There, I faced my old wounds head-on for the last time and gave them all up to Jesus. I recognized that because he had died on the cross for the wrong things I'd done, I needed to forgive myself, just as he'd forgiven me. His healing power won out in the end. I could hardly wait to get back and share the good news of God's love with my friends.

I began praying with other guys in my unit, encouraging them, just as my friend had me. I was surprised at how many responded positively. Being in the Marines could be lonely at times, but as I reminded them, with God, we were never truly alone. I spoke gently and patiently, and as time went on, God helped me grow more confident with my words.

Little did I know that God was preparing my heart to share his love with someone else hundreds of miles away. Though I had just embarked on an adventure halfway around the world, the real adventure was yet to come.

ॐॐॐ

going the distance

I was born in Steamboat Springs, Colorado, in 1984. My father, a Navy man, moved our family to The Dalles, Oregon, when he got a job on the Columbia River. He was a gruff man, protective and stern, and he always made me feel safe. My mother occasionally dragged me and my three sisters to the local Catholic church on Sunday mornings. But when softball season rolled around in April, church went by the wayside, and sports became the primary focus. I was especially athletic, and softball, basketball and soccer kept me busy for years. After graduation, I received an athletic scholarship to Mount Hood Community College in Gresham, Oregon. There, I played softball and ran cross-country. With my focus on sports and my studies, I had no time for boyfriends. My future seemed fairly secure and predictable. But my world was about to be shaken.

In 2005, after my second year of college, I moved back home with my parents. On the Fourth of July, some old high school friends invited me to a pool party. When I arrived at the house, I discovered that though there was plenty of booze, none of the guys' girlfriends were there.

"Where are the girls?" I asked them, scanning the backyard.

"Oh, they'll show up later," they returned, their voices already slurred.

I grew leery as the minutes ticked by and the girls failed to show up. As the guys continued to down the booze, they slowly encroached on me and began touching me inappropriately. I cringed as their hands went places I knew they shouldn't go. Though my mind raced frantically, trying to come up with an escape plan, I realized I was powerless beneath them. I was just one girl, and there were four of them. Despite the horror, I decided it was best to not put up a fight.

I returned home that night, sick to my stomach over what had just transpired. I felt dirty and disgusted at how my trusted friends had taken advantage of me. I contemplated telling my parents but knew my father would fly into a rage if he discovered what they'd done. Instead, I kept the shameful secret to myself and tried to get on with life.

A week later, my sister called one day and told me about a position for a park ranger in Culver, located over the mountain in Central Oregon. Eager for a change of scenery, I decided to apply and landed a job working the nightshift. There, I met another ranger named Mitch. He showed interest in me right away, and we soon began dating. Not long after our relationship took off, I noticed his subtle, controlling behavior. I made the mistake of sharing the Fourth of July incident with him, and he was especially intrigued by it.

"We should try a threesome sometime," he suggested, his eyes wide with curiosity.

"I don't know about that," I stammered. "I'm not really into that kind of stuff."

"C'mon. If you really loved me, you'd do something like that," he pressured.

The following month, I began e-mailing a guy named

going the distance

Ben on MySpace. I'd connected with my old neighbor Brad a couple years before, and he talked often about his friend Ben. I enjoyed my conversations with Ben. He was easy to talk to, and I found his work as a Marine interesting and admirable. We exchanged stories about our daily lives, and he always encouraged me. We shared a similar sense of humor and enjoyed swapping silly jokes. I smiled each time his "good morning" greeting popped up on my screen.

Ben talked often about his faith in God. In February, he shared that he had started leading small Bible study groups at his church. I was impressed with his devotion to God and his church but wasn't much interested in that for myself. The church I'd attended as a kid hadn't left an especially great impression on me, and I was in no hurry to dive into any religious stuff.

In March, Mitch tried again to talk me into swinging with another couple. Tired of hearing him discuss the subject, I finally gave in, and we engaged in a drunken sexual encounter at our house one night. I was repulsed by the whole thing, but Mitch continued to talk about how great it was.

"We should do that again," he said after it was all over.

Mitch had a way of sucking me in with his manipulative persistence, and I wasn't so sure I'd be strong enough to say no next time.

Mitch wasn't just interested in swinging — he was interested in everything sexual. From porn videos to strip clubs, Mitch wanted to try it all. He also talked of marriage, but at 21, I didn't feel anywhere near ready for that.

"Why don't we start small? Get a dog?" I suggested.

Mitch liked the idea. We got a cute little Weimaraner named Gob, and he became the center of our lives. But Mitch's controlling behavior worsened. He drew me in with his words of affirmation and then spit me out when I tried to speak up. I quickly learned that it was best to just nod my head and go along with his whims.

Ben and I continued our online friendship. Later in 2006, he told me he was deploying to Iraq again. He was excited to go, and I told him I'd be thinking of him while he was away. He promised we'd still be able to communicate while he was overseas.

In May 2007, Mitch talked me into another swinging party. Again, I downed the booze and went along with things, but after the encounter, my insides rolled. Deep inside, I wasn't sure Mitch was the guy for me. I'd grown weary of his behavior, but he professed to love me deeply, and I wasn't sure how to let go.

I graduated college and debated whether to stay in Portland or move to be near Mitch.

"You have to move near me," Mitch pressured. "Gob is a country dog, and he'll do great on my rural property."

I contemplated his words. *Perhaps I could get a waitressing job or something by his house,* I mulled. *I guess we could give it a try, and see if it works out.*

My father, who had not voiced his opinion about our relationship the entire time we'd been dating, approached me one day with some firm words. "Katie, I can't let you go be with Mitch. If I were you, I wouldn't let that guy near me."

His words cut deep. Despite his gruff ways, I knew my father loved me and wanted what was best for me. What was I to do?

A short time later, one of my sisters, six years older than me, wrote me a letter. "This guy is distancing you from your family," she wrote, expressing her dire concern. *She's right*, I realized. *Mitch is not a great guy. He's had me under his spell for too long, and it's time for me to get away from him once and for all. I've gotta figure out a way to leave.*

Ending my relationship with Mitch would be no simple task. Not only was he a big guy, but he also had a concealed weapons permit and kept firearms in his car. Though I'd never truly believed he'd hurt me, I also knew he had an angry streak. If I told him goodbye, would he try to harm me or my family? The thought made me shudder.

I spent the next month hatching a plan. After landing a job as a graphic designer in Hood River, Oregon, I decided to leave Mitch for good. I packed up Gob but left all of my other belongings at his house. I knew Mitch loved Gob and would be angry to find him gone, but he had already taken enough from me — my sense of security, my self-worth, my voice. I programmed 911 on my phone, just in case an emergency situation arose, and I left my two-year relationship behind.

As expected, Mitch called me a few days later. I had

just left for work at my new job when I picked up the phone.

"I'm coming tonight, and I want to talk to you," he told me firmly.

I tried to keep my voice calm and steady as I replied. "Okay, well, we can figure things out then."

I called my father to let him know Mitch would be coming that night. "There's nothing I can do to stop him," I said with a sigh. "I'll try to reason with him, and hopefully he'll just be cool and leave me alone. Will you have Mom put Gob in the backyard, just in case he tries to go after him?"

Mitch arrived that evening. I walked outside and met him on the porch, while my father watched from the front window. "Hi, Mitch." I forced a smile, hoping to appease him.

"I want to talk to you, but I can't talk here. Can we go for a walk?" he asked.

I glanced back nervously at the front window, where my father still huddled inconspicuously.

"Um, sure, I guess," I stammered. *I have friends just around the corner if I need to run for help,* I reasoned. *Plus, my dad won't let anything happen to me. It will be fine.*

We started down the street, and I cleared my throat and spoke up. "Mitch, I left for a reason. I don't want anything to do with you anymore. I'll get you back the rest of your stuff, and we can both move on, okay?"

Mitch's eyes were fiery as he glared at me under the

fading summer sun. He tried to argue back, but I remained firm.

"I'm done, Mitch, okay?" I turned on my heel and began to walk away. My heart thumped wildly beneath my shirt, and every inch felt like a mile as I sped up my pace and headed back toward the house. As I reached the porch, I pushed open the front door and tried to shut it, but Mitch, close on my heels, yanked it back open. To my horror, Gob had escaped from the backyard and was now at the front door. Mitch snatched him up and clutched him to his chest. Gob strained under his grip, and I watched, helpless and terrified.

As Mitch ran off, my father flew out the door and chased after him.

"Don't get in the car!" my mother screamed. She turned to me and told me she'd already called the police. They were on their way.

The cops careened around the corner, sirens blaring, and managed to stop Mitch a few blocks away. The next few minutes were a whirlwind as they escorted him back to the house. Mitch and I relayed our sides of the story.

"You guys can settle this now, or you can settle it in court," one of the cops told us. "What's it gonna be?"

I turned to Mitch, summoning all the calmness I could muster. "You know Gob is my dog. Just let him stay with me, okay?" I pleaded.

Reluctantly, Mitch agreed to hand over Gob. I knew he was very angry, and I hoped I had not just woken a sleeping bear. Mitch left, the officers left and I went inside, my heart still thudding as I tried to fall asleep. *Why did all this happen to me?* I wondered, bewildered, shaken and upset. *What did I do to deserve this sort of treatment? I'm not a bad person! This isn't fair!*

I remained on edge for the next few weeks, wondering if Mitch would have the nerve to contact me again. He called me a few times, but I ignored his attempts and changed my phone number. He then e-mailed me to tell me he wanted to send a care package to Gob. I was not impressed by the gesture. I just wanted him to go away. I changed my e-mail address as well, hoping to put this whole nightmare to rest.

I continued chatting with Ben, exchanging friendly banter, but inside, a piece of me died. After finally climbing off the emotional roller coaster I'd ridden with Mitch, I had no idea where to turn. When a friend invited me to a luau in July, I accepted, hopeful for a little fun in the midst of my depression. I drank too much that night, and thus, a new pattern evolved. I spent the next few weeks drinking myself into a stupor, convinced there was nothing to live for. As the booze flowed easily, I shoved aside my pain, trying to forget the horror of that Fourth of July party two years before, as well as my relationship with Mitch. *Screw it all,* I thought bitterly.

One August night, after drinking too much again, I messaged Ben online and gave him my phone number. He wrote back shortly, pointing out that I'd only given him six of the seven digits. I giggled, and he agreed to text me.

"I'm going to Hawaii for Brad's wedding, and right

now I'm sitting on a jet plane in California," he told me. "I've got some time to kill here."

Ben and I texted back and forth for the next two and a half days, and for the first time, I truly opened up to him. Though I'd shared casual, funny stories with him before, I'd never divulged much about my past. His gentle, kind demeanor helped me become vulnerable, however, and soon I found myself spilling all my feelings to a guy I'd never met.

"It sounds like you're really struggling to find peace," Ben said thoughtfully. "I know how that feels. I've been there myself. But God is the only one who can bring that peace."

I was glad he was not there in person to see me roll my eyes. I still didn't understand what the big deal was with this church and God stuff. "If there really is a God, why would he let all these bad things happen to me?" I pressed.

"Good question. Lots of people want to know the same thing." Ben went on to explain how God could take any situation and use it for good. God was not the author of evil, but in fact the author of goodness and life. Trusting that God knew best was the only way to find true peace.

I still admired Ben's faith, but I wasn't sure it was for me. How could I give my life up to a God I'd never seen face to face? How could I know for sure that he was real and good? What if it was all just a sham, much like my relationship with Mitch had been?

I found our old King James family Bible and began reading the first book, Genesis, determined to sort out this stuff once and for all. Though the version was confusing to read, my curiosity was piqued. I really did want to know more about this God Ben spoke of. *What if the Bible is really true and not just some elaborate hoax?*

The battle continued to wage in my mind. I did not want Ben to push his religion on me, but at the same time, I was intrigued by a God who loved us so much that he'd sent his son, Jesus, to die for the things we'd done wrong in our lives. I'd always assumed I would go to heaven because I was a decent person, but what if I was missing a huge chunk of the puzzle? I wasn't ready just yet to dive into this relationship with God Ben talked about, but I wasn't ready to walk away from the conversation, either.

New Year's Eve, I went to Newport Beach, Oregon, with some friends and partied my brains out, downing enough booze to help me completely forget my miseries back home. As the sun settled over the water and the waves crashed onto the rugged shore, I stared out at the ocean in my drunken state. My friends sat just a few feet away, their carefree laughter echoing down the beach. My stomach began to churn, and emptiness enveloped me.

I'm done with this lifestyle.

There's no point to it.

I've got to make a change.

But with no boyfriend, no purpose and no future plans, what was I supposed to do?

I woke up the next morning with a bad hangover and a sense of clarity. *I need to get myself to church,* I decided.

I showed up at church, a few weeks later, feeling

going the distance

slightly out of place as I took my seat in the very back. I recognized several familiar faces amongst the 200 people. I'd grown up with some of them, and the pastor had lived down the street from me when I was younger. I didn't talk to anyone that day but instead simply observed. To my surprise, I enjoyed the service more than I thought I would and decided I'd visit again the next week.

In December, Ben and I discussed meeting face to face. He was on leave and would be in the Washington area. The idea of seeing him in person after talking for so long online and over the phone was both exciting and intimidating. I wondered if he'd look like his picture — handsome, dark-haired and broad-shouldered. I was sure he had questions about me, too.

"You can come up and stay at my parents' house," Ben suggested. "They've got plenty of room."

I agreed to the visit, trying to tame the butterflies in my stomach as the big day approached. *I like this guy,* I decided. *I don't know where things are heading, but I really like him.*

I had no idea the wild ride I was about to embark on.

Ben was about to rock my world.

ॐॐॐ

I stepped off the plane and watched as the military wives raced forward to greet their husbands. While they exchanged overdue hugs and kisses, I stepped back and quietly observed. I had no one to come home to, no homemade dinner sitting in a Crock-pot back at the house or even a dog to lick my face when I walked in the door. And for the first time since joining the Marines, I realized just how lonely the military life could be.

My second deployment to Iraq had been much different than the first, and I was not quite prepared for my assigned tasks. I worked 12-hour nightshifts, slept all day and did not see the sun for two months straight. Our unit was attached to an aircraft carrier, and we spent part of our nearly 10-month deployment traveling all over the world. After making stops in Singapore, India, Australia and Afghanistan, we were finally ready to return to the States. I was seasick, but more than that, I was homesick.

Katie and I continued to talk during my deployment, and I grew to like her more and more. She was feisty and funny and shared my sense of humor. We swapped photos of our surroundings. She sent me pictures of the two feet of snow near her house, while I sent her pictures of the blazing winter sun in Iraq. I believed she wanted to take our relationship to the next level, but I was not ready to do that. As much as I cared about her, I knew she had not given her heart over to God, and I wanted a Christian partner more than anything. I decided to keep praying for her and let God take over the rest.

When I returned to Washington on leave, I invited Katie up to meet me and stay with my parents. I was thrilled when she agreed to come. The night before we met up, we got in a fight, but we worked things out, and I counted the minutes until our first face-to-face encounter.

going the distance

Slender with short strawberry-blond hair and piercing blue eyes, Katie was even prettier in person. She stared at me for a moment, as though trying to make sure I was real. We went to dinner and a movie and placed bets on who was going to win the UFC match. Our conversation flowed easily and continued that way for the next several days we spent together.

It's as if we were meant to be together all along, I told myself.

"I have something for you," I told Katie. I presented her with a four-disc CD series from my church. Each CD focused on a specific question, such as "Is the Bible real?" and "Am I on the road to heaven?"

"I hope these might clear up any questions you have about God," I told her.

"Thanks. I'll check them out. That reminds me ... guess what? I bought a Bible!" Katie said excitedly, pulling it out to show me. "I stopped at a Christian bookstore on the way here and got it. I think it was on clearance because it has red lettering throughout it."

I laughed. "Oh, that's not a mistake. The red lettering is the part where Jesus is speaking," I explained.

"Oh." She laughed in return. "That makes more sense."

During our time together, I talked to Katie more seriously about God. She still had many questions, and I wanted to answer them the best I could.

She shared she had been going to the college and career group at a local church and that she was starting to get to know people.

"That's great!" I affirmed her. "Having a church to belong to is so important."

"So are we going to start dating?" Katie pressed as our time together came to a close.

"I can't date you," I told her quietly. "You are not a Christian." I did not want to pressure Katie. I wanted to gently share God's love with her, just as my friend had done with me. I knew God was working on her heart, and I believed that in his timing she would be ready to invite him into her life.

Katie returned to Oregon and continued going to church. On January 1, she called me with wonderful news. "I invited God into my life, Ben! I get it now. It all just makes so much sense. I'm so excited!" She went on to explain how she'd listened to the discs I'd given her. At first she'd been reluctant and skeptical, determined to prove to me that this religious stuff was just some man-made way to get money and present the world with "feel good" material. But as she continued to listen to them, something subtly shifted inside. She let her guard down and realized that perhaps my pastor really did have something to say. And she began to wonder, *Would someone as radical as this guy really be a follower of God if this wasn't the truth?* God had gently tugged at her heart, and she had surrendered to him.

"That's great!" I gushed. I couldn't have been happier. Nor could I think of a better way to kick off the New Year. While we were still two different people, we now shared the most important thing on earth — our faith in God.

going the distance

In February, Katie and I decided to officially start a long-distance relationship. While she would remain in Oregon for now, I'd stay in Yuma and continue with my military duties. And we'd see where things went from there.

"I need you to know something," I told Katie one night as we talked. "You are never going to be number one in my life."

"What do you mean?" Katie asked, confused.

"Well, if I love you first, where does God fit in? I will love you best if I put God first."

Katie wasn't initially happy with my explanation, but I assured her that our relationship would only work if I focused on my relationship with God first. With his guidance, I'd be able to love her the way she deserved to be loved.

Katie continued to go to church, but she shared that her mother was skeptical about her new relationship with God. "I don't think she gets all this stuff," she told me. "I'm new to all this, so I'm not really sure what to tell her. I think she's unhappy I'm not going to the Catholic church. But she's asking questions, so I guess that's a good thing."

I continued to pray for Katie and her mother. I knew firsthand that having support and encouragement from others who loved God was so important. Meanwhile, I began to contemplate my own support system. I was a very good Marine and had a strong reputation. I knew I could have a successful career if I stayed in the military, but I knew it could also be a difficult life with a family. I wanted to pursue God first and foremost, but I also wanted to pursue a future with Katie. In March 2008, I decided to get out and follow my heart.

It was time to see how the next chapter unfolded.

࿐࿐࿐

I closed my new Bible and hopped out of bed, ready to start the day. The chilly Oregon rain had started to subside, and the sun had finally begun to poke out from behind the clouds. Spring brought with it the promise of new beginnings, as flowers burst into color and trees blossomed all over the valley. And much like this new season, a new season in my life was unfolding, bringing with it the promise of hope and healing.

In April 2008, I decided to go to Yuma for the Encounter at Ben's church. He had told me all about it, and it sounded like a wonderful way to strengthen my new faith. I was excited to see Ben, but I was looking forward to what the weekend had in store.

Roughly 70 other people from his church joined me at the Encounter that weekend. On Friday night, we gathered together and watched a video discussing Jesus' death on the cross. The next morning, we began at 6 a.m. with a time of worship and a daily devotion. I had never done a devotion before, but the leaders explained that it was a simple but special way to pray, read the Bible and journal about the thoughts God had put on our heart.

We spent some time filling out a survey about the

things we'd struggled with in our past. I knew I still struggled with guilt over my past relationships and experiences, and I wrote everything down as honestly as possible. As the leader prayed, she asked us to rip up the list we'd just finished filling out. I was confused, wondering why she'd wasted our time.

"All those things from your past need to be thrown away. The Bible says that if we invite God into our life, we are given a new heart. We are new creatures in him."

Ah, that makes sense. I shredded my paper, understanding the illustration. For the first time, I fully grasped God's powerful, redemptive love. I realized that even though I had not always made the best choices, it was not my fault that I'd been sexually abused by my friends and controlled by Mitch. As I released my pain to God, the chains that had been entangling me suddenly fell off, and an unexplainable peace washed over me.

I am made new in Jesus Christ. The truth was wonderfully freeing.

We broke into a time of deep prayer, and several leaders prayed over me. Again, I was filled with a wave of peace. I'd spent so long fighting the whole religious aspect of Christianity, but I now understood it wasn't about rules, but instead was about a lasting relationship with God. I'd been so focused on my friends and family judging me, still desperate to fit in and be accepted. But I had taken a new path now, and I could only hope and pray that they would see God in my life and join me on this journey someday.

shattered

I walked away from the weekend convinced that this was where I needed to be. I was excited about God, and I was ready to start a new life in Yuma with Ben.

"I want to move to Yuma," I told Ben after returning to Oregon. I'd helped Ben move out of the barracks during my trip down, and I knew he was ready to start the next chapter of his life, too.

Ben headed to Oregon in June and helped me pack all my things and stuff them in a U-Haul. I was grateful he'd taken such a liking to Gob. It was important to me that they got along. Gob climbed into the U-Haul next to me, and we made the long trip south. It was time to see if Ben and I had what it took to make a life together.

I'd forgotten how barren and hot Yuma was. It was the dead of summer when we arrived, and the sun beat down on me as I climbed out of the U-Haul and surveyed my new surroundings. For a moment, I grew wistful, thinking of the lush green mountains and valleys I'd just left behind. *But Ben isn't in Oregon,* I reminded myself. *He's here, and that's why I'm here now, too.*

Ben helped me settle into a little apartment on the second floor of the building. With no trees around for shade, the place looked a bit forlorn and desolate. Ben returned to work at his new job, and I tried my best to busy myself despite the climbing temperatures. *Oh, boy. I hope I made the right decision,* I thought, my mind again wandering to my home in Oregon. Would Ben and I have what it took to make our relationship last now that we were finally together?

going the distance

The days marched by, and slowly, I acclimated to my new life in Arizona. I enjoyed attending church with Ben and loved having hours to spend with him each day. Instead of chatting online, we now sat on the couch and talked until our eyelids grew heavy. I fell harder for Ben with each passing day, convinced we were meant to be together. Ben, in turn, told me the feelings were mutual. We officially began courting and planning our future together.

In August, we bought a house together using the money Ben had saved from his deployment. It was a foreclosure and needed quite a bit of work, but it was a great starter home. Ben, wanting to get me out of my seedy apartment, moved me in and then went to live nearby. We wanted to do things God's way and avoid temptation by not living together. Things were progressing quickly, but they just felt right. As our feelings grew stronger by the day, we began to discuss marriage more seriously. Little did I know that Ben had a very special surprise up his sleeve.

చాచాచా

This is the girl for me.

As Katie's face popped into my mind, a huge smile spread across my face. Like fine wine, our relationship had only grown better over time. What had started off as a fun friendship had turned into true love. I adored Katie's spunky, outgoing personality. We loved joking around, but I also appreciated her serious side, too. Katie hadn't just done the religious thing to impress me, but instead, she had truly sought out answers for herself. I loved seeing her grow in her new relationship with God. And I could hardly wait to spend the rest of my life with her.

I selected an engagement ring and showed up at the jewelry shop one afternoon to pick it up. As I spoke with the sweet older lady at the counter, a rough-looking guy sauntered in with a silver chain he wanted to pawn. The woman said something to me, but the guy thought she'd spoken to him.

"What the h*** did you say?" he shot off at her. As he continued to curse at her, the woman stared at him with wide eyes.

"Hey, man, she wasn't talking to you. She was talking to me," I intervened. I kept my voice steady, not wanting to start a fight.

To my shock, the guy pulled up his baggy pants, stormed over to me and spit in my face. Though my blood boiled, I kept calm as I continued to speak with him. "Look, man, let's be cool," I urged him.

At last, the guy backed off. "I'm really sorry, man," he said. "It's all good, okay?"

The adrenaline drained from my body as I walked out the door with my ring. *Thank you, God,* I prayed. *You helped me really stay calm in there.* I thought back to the angry kid I'd once been, ready to pick a fight with anyone who even looked at me wrong. Because I now understood God had a good plan for my life, I no longer felt the need to rack up meaningless accomplishments. My anger had been replaced with a true peace and joy that only came from above.

While Katie was out of the house, I painted "Will you marry me?" on the wall in the back room of our new house. Because we were in the middle of painting the wall, the idea seemed perfect.

I spread out rose petals on the floor and wrote a note telling her to come back to the bedroom. I then went and picked her up from Bible study. As we headed home, I began to panic, realizing my little plan might not work. *How am I gonna get back in the house before her? I've got to stall her.*

"Hey, my stomach is killing me. I'm gonna run in ahead of you," I told her quickly as we pulled up at the house.

"Don't you want to grab your laptop in the backseat?" Katie asked.

"Nah, I'll get it later." I ran inside and grabbed the ring. I heard Katie wander into the kitchen while I huddled in the back room, anxiously waiting. *Why is she taking her time? Doesn't she see the sign?* At last, when she still didn't come back, I called out, "Didn't you see the sign?"

"Yes, coming." At last, Katie entered the room. Her eyes grew wide as she read the words on the wall. "Yes, I'll marry you!" She ran and threw her arms around me.

I slipped the ring on her finger, and we sipped champagne from red Solo cups and celebrated.

shattered

Not wanting to wait any longer to be together, we married two weeks later in a small ceremony at the church. Only 12 people attended, including my boss. It was simple but sweet, just the way we wanted it. We decided to have a large reception with our families when we got back to the Northwest.

Katie and I celebrated our first Christmas together and settled into married life. Not long after we said our vows, she expressed to me that she was a bit homesick and didn't feel connected at the church.

"I've been going to the Bible studies and everything, but I just don't feel like I belong," she lamented.

We continued to pray, asking God for direction for the next season of our lives. I was happy with our church and our current lives, but I wanted Katie to be happy, too.

In August 2009, my company approached me with a promising opportunity on the border of Oregon and Idaho. I flew up to the area to check it out and liked it. Katie and I packed our stuff, put our newly remodeled house up for sale and headed back to the Northwest where we'd both come from. We moved into a tiny place in a rundown neighborhood, and I settled in at my new job.

Our first year of marriage proved challenging. I often rose at 3 a.m. for work and did not return home until 4:30 p.m. Exhausted, I headed to bed a couple hours later, only to wake up and do it all again. Though we saw little of each other, we remained convinced that this was where God wanted us. We found a new church, and not long after joining, the leaders asked if we'd consider working with the youth. Excited for an opportunity to serve, we agreed.

In April 2011, we stepped down as youth leaders, and I took up the role of an adult Sunday school leader. It amazed me to think back on my journey, realizing that just a few years before I'd been a lost, angry Marine, searching for answers. Now I had the amazing opportunity to share God's love with others everywhere I went.

Katie got a job in graphic design, and that summer, we started leading a group of young adults in a Bible study, focusing on reaching out to those who'd never heard about God or wanted to know more. One of Katie's coworkers invited her to a night of worship at another church when I was out of town one week, and she agreed to go. When I got home, she told me all about it.

"Everyone was so warm and welcoming, and the music was really upbeat and great," she told me. "I wouldn't mind checking it out again."

"I don't really want to leave where we're at," I replied reluctantly.

I agreed to attend a barbecue with some people from the other church one day, however, and just as Katie had said, everyone was extremely welcoming. *Maybe this is a really good fit for us,* I thought. As with everything in life, I took the decision to God in prayer. Meanwhile, I got promoted at work, and we moved to a better area. We thanked God for providing all our needs. Trying to sell our house back in Yuma had proven especially challenging and living in dumpy places had been frustrating, but our patience finally paid off. Once again, we waited and prayed, wondering what adventure would come next.

❧❧❧

"I'm so glad you came over." Renee smiled at me warmly as we stepped inside their house. Their children ran around, playing happily at their parents' feet.

Pastor Doug and his wife, Renee, sat with Ben and me for the next four hours, sipping coffee and discussing life with us. We shared our story with them, and they shared theirs. I felt right at ease, so thankful to not have to put on a perfect face in front of them. I'd always been a bit feisty and outspoken, and I worried sometimes that my words might not come out right to others. But they were so easygoing that it felt as if we were long-lost friends. *They're real people just like us, with crazy lives and appointments and schedules.*

"As soon as we met you, we really felt strongly that God was doing a special work in your lives," Pastor Doug told us. "We really feel that a couple like you would have great ministry opportunities as a part of our church."

I wonder what they need us for? I thought. *We're just a couple of newlywed kids from Yuma, Arizona.* But the words were flattering all the same.

I chatted and hung out with their youngest daughter for a bit before we left. For the first time in a very long while, I felt as though I'd come home. *This just feels right.*

going the distance

I think Christian Life Fellowship could really be the place for us.

In February 2012, Ben and I made the move to Christian Life Fellowship. It felt so good to finally have a place to belong. The church focused heavily on sharing the good news of God's love with everyone, something we both believe is very important. We knew there were many more people just like us who'd either never heard about God or had misconceptions about him. Many, including ones I'd met at work, had questions just as I once had. They were skeptical, confused and convinced that this whole religious stuff just wasn't for them. But I hoped that our stories could help them see that having a relationship with God was the most exciting and important decision they'd ever make in their lives.

❧❧❧

"That looks great! You made that?" I stepped back to admire Katie's handiwork.

"Yep. You like it?" She smiled.

"I love it."

Katie had taken some old wooden pallets and had the words "As for me and my house, we will serve the Lord" written on them. I was excited to put it up on the wall of our new house. It would be a good reminder to all who walked in that Katie and I put God first in our home.

We settled in front of the TV for the latest football game, Gob settling contentedly at our feet. I pulled Katie close, thankful once again for such an amazing wife. We had certainly been through our ups and downs in the past few years, but in the end, we'd only grown closer to each other and to God. As I reflected on my life, I couldn't help but be amazed at all God had done. He had taken a lost, angry kid and transformed me into a man after God's own heart. He'd given me purpose and joy, two things I'd once feared I'd never find.

Katie, in turn, had transformed from a skeptical young girl into an amazingly Godly woman. I loved watching her grow in her relationship with God and sharing him with others. She now had a positive outlook on life that others found contagious. Though she'd once set out to prove me wrong about religion, she'd discovered God's beautiful plan for her life in the process. And in the midst of it all, I'd fallen head over heels in love with her.

In the end, we were not so different from one another after all. We were just two kids from the Northwest, once separated by 1,200 miles as our lives took us down different paths. We were both broken, lonely and lost, but thanks to God, we were both restored. As our worlds intersected, our hearts and lives meshed, and we discovered that we were better together. Our relationship had gone the distance, but the rest of the adventure is yet to come.

dancing to the clouds
The Story of Cyndee Orcutt
Written by Holly De Herrera

"We have to move. We'll be gone a long time." Betty, the only mom I had ever known in this life, was leaving. Years before, my first mom had decided it was best for me to live with my dad after their divorce. Now it was happening again. Betty was looking me in the eye like she wanted to say something. I imagined the words all jammed up inside her throat blocking a whole ocean of things she needed to tell me. Instead she just said, "I'll miss you." Did I imagine the thin line of tears in her eyes trying to find its way up?

"But why? Can't you take me with you?" My voice seemed so small and weak. Smaller than the miniscule buttercups hanging grieving heads over the patches of grass. Smaller than the tiny stones under my feet and definitely smaller than the words I wanted so badly to say. I cleared my throat hoping that would help. Maybe if I just said the right thing, she wouldn't leave. But what could I say? She had made up her mind.

My half-sister, Jenn, grabbed my hand and seemed to muster all of her 6-year-old courage before adding, "I don't want to go. I want to stay here. With Cyndee. And Dad. And you."

Betty shook her head, said, "Impossible," then reached

for Jenn, her real daughter, and lifted her up against her chest. She gave me one last look and whispered into Jenn's dirty-blond head, "I'm sorry. You have to come with me." I secretly wished she would lift me up, too, and at least put up a fuss on my account. At least so the terrible pit in my stomach wouldn't twist and turn so much.

Later, I watched from my upstairs bedroom, pressing my hands and forehead against the window, and tried to be brave and swallow down the thick lump in my throat. I focused hard on my most favorite things. Dancing. Twirling on an open stage. But it didn't help. The sky and the trees all agreed with me that this day was sad. The saddest day I'd ever known. All the expanse above my house looked flat and iron-grey, and if I didn't know better, I'd have guessed that was all there was. No blue and certainly no sunshine. Ponderosa pines reached their lanky arms up, needles prickling into the air like they were begging for something. The enormous boulders that surrounded the bottom of the house seemed to lift me up and away from my mom and sister, walling joy out, hiding it away in some mysterious cove where sometimes I'd go in my mind's eye to dance into a rainbow. But that wasn't real. Nothing was real anymore. Most especially love.

Betty's tiny black and yellow car wound down the driveway like a bumblebee going home after a long day's work. Only she wasn't coming back. She was flying off to New Zealand, wherever that was, and making a new home with Jenn where I wasn't invited to join them. I watched until she was just a fleck of yellow against grey. And then,

dancing to the clouds

a second later, she was gone, swallowed up by the grey. As though her yellow light had never really been here at all.

க்க்க்

No one can convince you that you're wanted once you start believing you're not. It's just a part of you, like your eyes or your blond hair — a part of how you see the world and how the world sees you. But that didn't keep me from pretending for a while. When I was 16, I lived with a friend and her mom in an apartment. We were pretty much on our own all the time. Together, we pretended that we were grown and didn't need anyone. I pretended I wasn't a girl with issues and enjoyed my escapes into mystical lands through drugs and alcohol. I let boys love me for a while just because it filled that hole where I'd hide when pretending didn't work anymore. In between, I found grounding in dancing. It was the only thing that felt beautiful and right.

None of the pretending kept me from true love, amazingly enough. I met Dusty at Pizza Hut. He washed the dishes, and I managed the restaurant. We became best friends first, taking off for the slopes to snowboard or finding some adventure together. Later I began to notice that he was different — not just after what he could get from me, like so many others. No, he was in my corner. Somehow I knew that. Like that comfortable feeling I'd get when it was just me on the dance floor. Nothing could get in the way of how right that felt, and the same was true with Dusty. He has always had a nice physique, and I'm not ashamed to say that I still enjoy looking at him. But mostly it was his loyalty I fell for. He is someone who would never leave, never give up just because things got hard. And they have gotten hard. Harder than I ever imagined that day we said, "I do."

When our first child was born, our little Zoe Jayne, Dusty and I were so excited and in love. She decided to arrive when she wanted, not when we expected.

I walked into the sterile examination room for my regular OB appointment and changed into a less-than-modest backless hospital gown. The nurse tapped lightly on the door, and I called, "Come in." She entered and offered a smile.

"We're going to check you, Mama. Let's see where you're at."

Dusty stood and reached for my hand as I lay back for the exam. Moments later the nurse looked at me, then at my husband, and said, "How about you have this baby today?"

"As in now?" My husband looked at the nurse, then at me. "As in we don't have time to go get our overnight bag, now?"

The nurse removed her rubber gloves with a snap. "You're dilated to eight. I think now is definitely the time. I'll go get the doctor, but let's move you to a delivery room right away."

And just like that our baby was born, blue eyes, pouty

lips and a round face with the softest blond baby hair. She was perfect in every way.

It was the small things we noticed. Things that didn't seem right. "Look." I signaled for him to come closer. "This is what I'm talking about. She shakes a little. Her head and her hand." He touched her hand with his large fingers, and she seemed to still for a moment, but then it would continue and happen at unexpected moments.

"Something's wrong. Let's just tell the doctor about it at her 6-month checkup."

I nodded, pressing my lips closed because I didn't dare voice any concerns for fear the words might take on a life of their own and become real. For now, it was just good not knowing. Pretending it was just a little thing she did. Like a personality quirk.

"Sure. I'll do that." I leaned down and brushed a kiss on her velvety head. "I love you to the moon and back," I whispered. Fear clogged my throat, stung my eyes and made me wonder what could be worse than having something terribly wrong with your baby. Dusty and I had waited to have kids. Not because we were against the idea, but because we just didn't feel compelled to do it. We had fun just being free and married, without worries. Well, mostly. We had uprooted and moved from Lake Tahoe to Wisconsin with nothing but a business idea. That had nearly killed me, or so I thought. And even more so when the business tanked with the economy and we didn't even have enough money to fix our broken heater. But compared to this wondering, that was a walk in the park.

I lifted little Zoe up to my chest, willing her to draw strength from me, and began to hum as she snuggled up against me. For a moment it was as though we were one person, with one heartbeat, one breath and one dream for a bright, full future, free of worry and sickness and pain.

"Cyndee." The doctor's voice on the other end sounded so grave, so whispery quiet compared to the sound of my car on the highway making the hour-long drive home from the hospital. "You need to come back in. Zoe's test results were abnormal. We're going to need to do some more tests."

"What?" My voice sounded shrill and weak, and I forced myself to swallow down the sick feeling that burned my throat. "What is it?"

"Just come back today, and we'll talk this through in person. Not on the phone, Cyndee."

"All right. I'm turning around now."

The hour back to the hospital felt like a drive to impending doom. The sky seemed to gather clouds together to mimic my mood. Where did that sunshine go again? I called Dusty to let him know, and he said he'd meet me there. I had to answer his questions with nothing but, "I don't know. They aren't saying. But I know it's not good. Otherwise, why would I have to come back this instant?"

"I'll get there as soon as I can." The steady way he said it made me calm just a little, like the center of a tornado. I knew the feeling would whip off into the sky with all the other false securities I had held on to. Like my own strength and Dusty's. Neither of us was prepared for what would come.

༄༄༄

"Angelman Syndrome. That's what the testing showed." The doctor leaned forward in her chair, her elbows on her knees and began again. "Zoe will need extra-special care and might have some developmental delays. She might seem different from other kids. The syndrome is associated with delays in speech and motor skills, and sometimes seizures are present."

"But can she live a full life? What is ..." My husband's voice trailed off, leaving the last words unsaid but fully clear. Would our baby girl grow and live past her childhood?

With a sympathetic smile, the doctor said, "People with this syndrome tend to live a regular lifespan, and I do believe she can live a very full, happy life. There can be complications caused due to seizures, but the syndrome itself isn't cause to expect anything less than what you'd expect for other kids without it. It's just a new way of looking at your daughter and helping her to thrive."

The feeling of pressure in my head throbbed steadily, but I only answered, "Well, then we will do everything we can to be the kind of parents she needs. But we'll need your guidance to know what to do. How to help her."

shattered

"Of course." The doctor stood and put a hand on my shoulder. "I believe you will do well, and so will Zoe."

My husband's normally steady reactions were betrayed by the way he opened and closed his hands and the flicker of muscle in his jaw moving, which was almost unperceivable. He nodded and reached for my hand. I knew he was telling me that we were in this together and that it didn't matter. We loved our Zoe Jayne just as much and maybe even more than we did before we found out about her needs. This was a battle cry, and nothing would get in the way of us doing what our girl needed. I stood, infused with new vision. My only question was how to fit all the love that seemed uncontainable. Like I needed a completely new heart to hold it all in.

ॐॐॐ

It was the day of the football playoff game, and friends were over watching on our big screen. Cheers went up like waves and then settled, followed by another outburst. Zoe played on the floor. She loved to roll around and explore the small world we had created for her in our living room. She was always in the center of everything we did, and today was no different. Though, at the moment, nobody was watching her.

Another yell and several screams of, "What are you doing?" The excitement thrilled our little girl. I could hear her soft "ahh, ahh." At the age of 2, she hadn't uttered a complete word but still found ways to communicate.

dancing to the clouds

Everyone who met her loved her. I got caught up in the game, tucked in beside Dusty, who was less than cozy to snuggle up to with his bouncing on the chair in response to the players. Movement out of the corner of my eye snatched my attention from the screen to where Zoe was.

"Dusty!" I pulled on his arm and added, "Look at Zoe!"

He leaned forward to see around me to where she had been and leaped to his feet. Our little girl was army crawling across the floor with slow, jerky movements, but she was doing it. Dusty moved to where she was and began cheering her on like a coach running beside a runner. With her wet mouth wide open and her arms reaching forward, she inched along, blue eyes fixed in determination on some imaginary goal. In moments all the guests had forgotten the game and began cheering, too, like she was the all-star and nothing else mattered but her. "Go, Zoe! You can do it!" And just like that I was reminded all over again that love celebrates in victories, no matter how small they might seem to the rest of the world. Our baby girl was crawling, and I knew then she could do anything.

పాపాపా

The dance studio where I worked was full of giggly girls all moving to the music. I pressed Zoe's back against my legs, her feet perched carefully on mine.

"Ah. Ah." She was happy. I could just tell when she felt

shattered

that deep down joy from something as beautiful as dancing. This was something she loved. This was a place she could let the music take her away, someplace I could only imagine. I moved her over to her walker and got her stabilized, and she took off from there, pushing it forward, moving her small legs forward and bouncing in her special way. Seeing her filled my chest with such a warmth, like someone had handed me the sunshine and said, "Here, this is yours."

For me, dancing has always been my hideaway and, at the same time, my full expression of myself, of my heart, my struggles, my fears, poured out like an offering. Every day after teaching my classes, I turned on one last song, the studio empty, and danced off the worries, frustrations, what ifs and agony of wondering whether my girl would ever be able to dance, too, without being held up by my arms or by a metal frame. Not that she seemed to mind, but I minded for her, knowing all that she should be able to enjoy. But my Zoe always did bring me back to earth and remind me that being just like everyone else isn't really what matters, anyway. Her open-mouthed smiles and kisses reminded me daily of the riches so many others would never get to experience with a "normal" child. Zoe was my hero. The reason I kept going and trying and remembering and loving.

"Ready to go see Daddy and your baby brother?" The only one she might have loved more than her daddy was her brother, Deaken. The two of them spent hours rolling around the floor, discovering new lands together.

dancing to the clouds

"Ah. Ah." I could see the wide-eyed way she responded and knew she could hardly wait. Dusty danced with Zoe ballroom-style, with her arm out with his, waltzing across the house. There was no shortage of love for our girl. If love could sustain a person, our Zoe would have lived forever.

৯৯৯

The cold Idaho winter had set in; pale tree trunks stretched on forever it seemed on our vineyard property out away from the city. Cold wind walked through the rows and snaked around the grass, now hay-yellow and dry. The leaves had long since fallen and mulched the dark soil.

The seizures began so heavy and unexpectedly. Why now? Why so all of a sudden when she had been doing so well? I felt sure she must be just growing and her meds needed adjusting. Blood work, testing and trial and error with new kinds of meds sent our new rhythm into a tailspin. Nothing made sense. The days at the hospital dragged like a punishment for Zoe. My heart ached watching her not responding and having to endure more and more. More than any 6-year-old girl should have to.

One cold morning she just didn't seem right. Her head, normally thrown back to look up at me, suddenly lolled to the side, like her neck couldn't handle the weight of it. My heart beat thick and full. I pulled her up against my chest and sang softly, "When I call on Jesus, all things are possible." In my mind we flew out the window together and found a cloud where we could ballet into the sky, away from the unknown and the pain. Away from everything I couldn't control and make better for my daughter.

But my little one was suffering. I could feel it in the way she held her little body, and I could tell she wasn't herself because she was quiet and lethargic. No soft "ahh," showing her world was all right. No, she was so terribly quiet.

Christmas came and went. Dusty and I tried to make it a joyful time, but it was like holding onto sand, the time felt so out of our control, out of our grasp. Zoe seemed weak and was losing weight since she couldn't keep food down.

It was January 18. Zoe had been taken by ambulance to another hospital because they knew that better care could be given there. A CT scan was scheduled, and Dusty and I wanted to be with her every step of the way. As we rolled her down the hall, I remembered how just months before she had been so vital. She looked just the same, curled up with a faint smile on her face. It seemed like hours before the doctor returned to share the results.

Were those tears in his eyes? His shoulders looked tired and sad. "Zoe has a massive malignant brain tumor. That's why everything has been happening." A group of nurses stood by crying.

I couldn't wrap my mind around what was happening. We had our answer. And now we could start planning. We would operate, and Zoe would be okay. Why did everyone look so defeated? I was ready to fight! My heart slowed some knowing my girl had hope.

"You'll need to speak with the neurosurgeon for the next steps." With that, he quietly exited the room. It was 2 a.m., and the on-call doctor had been woken from his rest to come in and give us those "next steps."

Still, in the back of my mind, I pressed back the thought, *Why tonight? Why not in the morning?*

I don't know how much time had passed. Minutes, hours, years? But the neurosurgeon did come, and he invited us to look at the X-ray of Zoe's brain on his screen. I scanned the picture looking for signs of a tumor. Every tiny dot and blob I momentarily thought was the tumor. They seemed small, and I felt confident we could remove the tumor and our girl would be able to heal and keep growing and living.

Suddenly, I saw it. It took up most of the back of her brain, and I could feel my chest tighten down. Dusty looked on quietly. I could tell he was processing just like I was and wondering how to save his baby.

"The tumor is about two and a half by three inches, and it's pressing on her brain stem," the doctor began. "There are a few options. We could operate, but Zoe would be unable to do a lot of things. You said she can walk with a walker and feed herself?"

I nodded. "Yes, she can." I felt so proud of her. I sat up just a little higher in the hard plastic chair.

"She wouldn't be the same. She wouldn't do those

things anymore, if she even survived the surgery. It's very invasive." I swallowed down the burning in my throat.

"What is the second option?" My husband's voice sounded gruff and exhausted.

"We can put in a shunt to reduce the pressure on the brain and possibly prolong her life, but not by much, I don't expect. And the surgery itself might be too much for her."

I waited for him to give the third option, but I couldn't make myself ask for it. My world felt like everything I cared about was escaping my grasp.

"Or you could take her home. You could enjoy these last few days of her life without any interference from us."

Days? Lightning exploded in my head, and somewhere far away I heard my husband ask, "How long?"

The doctor said in a near whisper, "Days. Five, maybe. I wouldn't anticipate more than a few weeks." Then he added, "I'm so very sorry."

And then my world crumbled. The whole place seemed like the inside of a cave, and there was no light to tell me which way to go. What to do next. I felt my heart throbbing, and I nearly gagged on the sob I held in. This wasn't how it was supposed to be. Zoe had a normal life expectancy, right? What had I missed? What had I done wrong? I was a nursing student. Why hadn't I known — been able to tell somehow? Questions tumbled down on me like boulders reminding me of my weakness and reminding me of my faith.

I felt the tidal wave of fear and anxiety and sorrow

tumbling over me. I felt Dusty pull me into him as I cried out, screamed out, "Why? Why? Why?" The doctor had left, and it was just us and a thick, slithering agony.

Dusty's tears pressed into my chest, deep gut-wrenching cries. "It's not fair! We have done everything right, and Zoe works so hard. Why is this happening to us?"

I didn't know the answer. I didn't know anything anymore. All I could say was, "I don't want her to go. What am I going to do without her? What am I going to tell her brother?"

Somehow, despite our deepest fears being realized, besides wanting desperately to hold on and watch her grow up, we knew what we had to do. Our baby was dying, and there was only one option for us. We were taking her home to get her ready to meet Jesus.

"Will you praise God in the storm or fall like so many others when tragedy hits?" The question taunted and buffeted me those last two weeks of Zoe's life.

God had gotten a hold of me two years after Dusty and I had married and after years of not caring, living for myself, trying to hide from anything that mattered and seeking comfort, hiding from rejection. I remember the day I got baptized in frigid Lake Tahoe. The sky was gloomy, and a brisk wind danced across the water. I pulled my sweater around me wondering what kind of idiot gets baptized in water cold enough to give her pneumonia. But then the sun broke through the clouds, blue spread out across the sky and I knew it was God telling me he loved me and to go ahead, take the dip of faith. As the icy water spread over my face and my hair spiraled up around me, I felt wrapped in love I had never known. My hot tears mixed with the cold lake water because for the first time I felt whole, like I was worth something. I felt completely loved, and I knew that God "had" me and would never leave me. He would never drive away and disappear into the grey. He loved me with a complete, selfless love, and I was worth his death on the cross. He died for the very people crucifying him. He died because his blood was the only perfect sacrifice able to take away the wrong things I'd done. And I know, though it happened 2,000 years ago, he died knowing I would need him to. I would be crying out his name in my darkest hours. He knew. He would have died that agonizing death even if it had just been me calling out for his saving grace.

But nobody told me then that life would be so hard. Nobody said I'd lose my baby girl and wonder why I was given such a perfect gift only to have it snatched away. Peace came somehow. I needed to let Zoe go be with the Lord. I knew deep down that holding on to her and putting her through the surgery wasn't what was best for her. No, this was my chance to lay my own longing down and choose what was right for my daughter. And just like that, determination hit like a gale force wind. I decided I would praise my God come what may and that I would cling to him, because I knew that if I didn't, I would be swallowed up by a sea of darkness and empty black despair.

dancing to the clouds

৵৵৵

We made Zoe a bucket list and quickly did all the things we thought she would love. We bundled her up in a pink snowsuit and took her sledding down a snow-covered hill. On another evening, we painted her twitchy little toenails with a pink Sharpie, just because nail polish would dry too slowly for how much she liked to move her legs around. One night we took her to our church, Christian Life Fellowship, because she always loved the music and always seemed so content there. She smiled in her sweet way, and a friend said she saw angels surrounding Zoe as the worship music played. Her last days, 14 to be exact, were filled with joy as we tried to savor our last moments with God's gift to us.

The end was drawing near, we could tell by how sleepy Zoe had become. A makeshift bedroom had been set up in the living room, and Zoe's grandmother had bought 20 balloons that filled the ceiling over the bed as our little girl gazed up at the colorful display. Pastor Doug from CLF came by regularly to pray with and just be there for us, and Pastor Jack Becker helped with Zoe's hospice care. On February 1, Dusty and I lay in bed with Zoe, her arms looped over our heads. She had such a look of contentment and joy. I sang softly, "Come and go with me to my father's house." She smiled and cuddled her daddy and me while we held on to her. Dusty slipped on her favorite baby boxing gloves, the ones she always loved to chew on, and kissed her face gently. At around 2:30 a.m., my beautiful girl slept peacefully, but I could tell she was ready to go home. I whispered against her pale skin, "I love you to the moon and back." The soft light in the room allowed me to see her just before she left us. "I'll miss you. You're going to do amazing things in heaven, I just know it. It's okay, angel, you can go be with Jesus. I'll meet you there later."

And then she was gone. She went to her father's house, danced off into the sky to him, unlimited and fully free to express her joy. Finally.

That next morning, I pulled up my Facebook page and wrote a tribute to my baby girl.

Worst day of my life (so far): At 2:30 this morning, my Angel was gone. She was way stronger than me! I will miss her glowing smile, her infectious laugh, her pulling my hair, biting my ears and the copious amount of drool that comes with a Zoe-bug hug!!! I will miss everything!

Best day of my life: I believe God sent his Son, Jesus, to die for our sins so if we believe in him we could have life eternal. I believe Zoe knew Jesus intimately, I believe Zoe is in heaven. She is running, skipping, dancing and singing at the top of her lungs!!! I CAN'T WAIT to hear that beautiful sound. God has his VERY BEST Angel now. I love you, Zoe!!

Pain doesn't adequately express what it is to lose a child. But I find hope and help as I walk through this. Just the other day I was at church; it was Mother's Day, and I almost felt I couldn't stand the terrible ache of missing my Zoe. The service was beginning, and I wondered if I would be able to make it through. A memory of Zoe danced in front of me. She was small and wearing a pink onesie and spotting a blue Mylar star-shaped balloon bobbing above her just out of reach. Zoe wobbled on her tummy a moment before reaching her chubby arm up and grabbing it, a smirk twisting her tiny drooly mouth. I could tell she had never been more proud of herself.

If only I could just hold her again, press her warm body against my chest and smother her in kisses. I bowed my head, tears clogging my throat and running hot down my cheeks. "Lord, I really need your help today; can you please give me some strength?" Looking up, I brushed back the tears and took a deep breath, something I did often in an attempt to pull myself together. And then I saw it, bobbing along the ceiling of the church sanctuary: a blue Mylar star-shaped balloon. I knew then that God was with me, encouraging me and reminding me that Zoe is safe and that just because she isn't here with me, she isn't gone, either. She is full of joy, laughing and dancing and talking a mile a minute. I just need to be patient and not forget when the lonesomeness threatens.

It was only a few months after Zoe's passing that I was asked to dance at CLF's women's retreat. I had mixed feelings. My heart seemed an unstable thing, and I wondered if I could really do justice to any performance that mattered. Sure I danced when I was alone, pouring

shattered

my heart out to God, allowing my journey to find expression in the movements. But this seemed too much, almost. Still, I've never been one to shy away from a challenge. "I'll do it." I put the firm answer out there before I could talk myself out of it.

The music began to play that first day of the retreat, a room full of women sitting quietly, watching from their safe perches around the room. My friend Joni began singing, and I allowed my dance to be for only one: God. I needed this to be for him. The words weaved through my movements, and I felt his nearness. "… And I know there will be days, when this life brings me pain, but if that's what it takes to praise you, Jesus, bring the rain." I pictured Jesus holding my little girl during that performance. I remembered that she was okay, and I only had to be patient because I knew I would be with her again someday.

∾∾∾

Dusty held Deaken in one arm, a bright yellow balloon in the other. "What do you want to say to her this time?"

"I want to say I miss her. And, also, what's she eating in heaven?"

I pulled the balloon down to my chest and wrote out his words with a Sharpie. "Good ones." I ruffled his head with my fingertips before we all took hold of the thin balloon string. This was our once-a-month ritual, our balloon talks with Zoe. "One, two, three!"

dancing to the clouds

We all watched it float slow and steady up into the sky, then shoot up more quickly with a sudden breeze.

Deaken kept watching, pulling his wubby, which was his thin, very loved blanket that we referred to as a "he," up to his cheek. "Wubby wants to be with sister."

"I know he does. We all do." Dusty's voice sounded like gravel under tires.

"We will be. When it's the right time." I needed my son to know the hope he could take hold of. The truth that death is not the end. Not for Zoe. Not for any of us.

The spot of yellow grew more pale against the brilliant cobalt-blue sky. It looked so small but, I suddenly thought, so brave. And before I could tell the difference between the yellow of the balloon and the yellow of the sunshine, it was gone. Blended in or maybe absorbed by all that light. No disappearing into grey. Just hope meeting up with hope. That's how God is. Always with us through every trial, every hurt. Never leaving, just loving us through it all. I imagine Zoe finding our balloon and dancing off to her father in heaven to tell him all about her mama and daddy and little brother. And I'm sure she is getting things ready for us. I just know it. Because that's my girl.

whole
The Story of John
Written by Arlene Showalter

"Get in here!"

I ran as fast as my 5-year-old feet could carry me. Fear gnawed at me as I skidded to a halt in my own bedroom. Dad glowered down at me.

"I told you to clean up your room."

I looked around for the reason of his rage this time. My bed was made and my sparse toys tucked away. I turned a blank face up to him.

"There!" he shouted. "Under the bed."

I got down on my hands and knees. Nothing. I searched harder. There, tucked behind one leg and against the wall, lay a lone sock. I shimmied to it on my belly and then rose to my feet, sock in hand.

"Stupid kid," Dad said, pulling off his belt. "Grab your ankles. I'll teach you to obey."

I bent over, but try as I might, I couldn't hold onto my ankles and maintain my balance. Finally, Dad grabbed my arm and flailed away at my backside.

"You don't have the brains God gave a goose," he panted between swings.

ॐॐॐ

shattered

Birth placed me in the middle of five children and with parents who circled one another like sharks. We kids lay in the middle of that bloody feeding ground.

My father pastored churches in our denomination and worked odd jobs on the side. His ego and inability to get along with others forced our family into frequent moves. Just about the time I began making friends, we'd be packing and relocating to a new home, church and city.

We'd moved to another small town during first grade. A fireplace and propane heater in the dinky living room provided our only sources of heat. The house lacked venting to carry the heat into the other rooms.

I looked at the pretty yellow flowers dotting our lawn. They seemed so cheerful against the dreary atmosphere of constant rain. *I'll take some to Mommy,* I decided. I collected a fistful and ran into the house.

"Here, Mommy," I said, holding out the happy flowers. "These are for you!"

"Those aren't flowers," she said, recoiling. "They're dandelions."

I stood there, uncertain.

"Throw them away!" she screamed. "They're nothing but weeds."

I scooted as fast as my 6-year-old legs could move and dumped them in the garbage along with my joy.

Later that year, Dad fell out with a prominent member of his church.

"What are you doing?" Dad demanded, when the man showed up at our house.

whole

"Propane tank belongs to me." He grinned. "So, I'm taking it — now."

The task of keeping our family warm fell to me. I swung the axe down, splitting the firewood piled before me. The work kept me outside, away from the screams and slaps that reverberated in the puny rooms.

Mrs. Cummings, my third grade teacher, called me to her desk after the rest of the students had left for the day. We'd moved again the year before.

"Please turn around, and take down your pants," she directed. "Just your outer pants, not your underwear." Her voice remained low, but firm. I stiffened. Boys in our home never, ever exposed themselves to any female, family or otherwise.

"Please." Her voice gentled.

I turned my back to her, loosened my belt and let gravity drop my pants. My cheeks burned.

Silence. I knew what she saw. Angry welts, like swollen red-coated soldiers, marched from my buttocks to my ankles.

"You can pull them up now," she said.

I did and turned around. Her eyes flashed with anger. I stepped back.

She's gonna kill me.

Mrs. Cummings took a deep breath and released it like a pricked balloon. "You can help me after school," she said, "as often and as late as you want."

Although she showed little outward affection, Mrs.

shattered

Cummings became my hero and her classroom, my refuge. When Dad beat the crap out of me, I pictured her face, standing at the window, observing. I knew she was on my team.

The only one on my team.

Dad beat me on a daily basis that year. He needed no *why* and never provided one.

"Grab your ankles." The familiar order rang in my ears. I bent over, but the moment I hopped around to avoid the blows, he screamed, "Dancing's a sin. Stop it!"

I couldn't.

"Take down your pants," he commanded. He figured if my feet got tangled in the dropped drawers, I'd stop committing the sin of dancing. When that failed to work, he gripped my arm and swung the belt every which way. He didn't care what part of my body he thrashed, as long as it was mine.

My parents attacked each other with the same ferocity as they beat their offspring.

"I'm leaving!" Mom yelled.

"Don't care if you do," Dad retorted. "I'll even help. Let me check and see if there's enough oil in the car."

From my window, I watched him jimmy the engine.

"It's good to go," he said, coming back into the house.

Mom stormed out and turned the key. Nothing. She stormed back in.

Mission accomplished.

What a stupid game, I thought.

whole

᪥᪥᪥

My parents had to pass through the bedroom I shared with my brother to get to their own. Many nights I lay in my bed, hearing their squabbles through the thin walls.

On Memorial Day weekend, I lay awake in bed, longing but not able to drown out the sounds of their discontent, while my younger brother slept beside me. My sisters were staying over at Mom's parents' house so they could help decorate the graves of my two uncles who'd died in the service.

"I want to go," Mom said. "Those are my brothers."

"Not going." Dad's tone was flat. "Come over here, and give me some sugar."

"No!" Mom screamed.

The arguing and screaming went on and on. Finally, Mom passed me to go to my sister's room and flounced on the empty bed. Minutes later, Dad followed, naked, and flipped on the light.

"Come on, Diane," he coaxed. "Give me some sugar."

She fought him off.

I lay in my bed, staring.

Dad looked up and saw me.

"Go to sleep!" he roared. He slammed the door shut.

A few minutes later, Mom threw the door open and moved to the living room. Dad followed. No longer in my line of vision, I listened to the scuffling and Dad making weird noises.

Then silence.

shattered

I quaked in the bed. *What did Dad do to Mom?*

"B*****d!" Mom's shriek split the air like my axe to firewood. I heard footsteps stamping to the garage and back.

Next, I heard Dad pleading, "No, Diane, no."

I heard the dull thud of board hitting flesh.

Mom hitting Dad? Why? Why? I lay in my darkened world — paralyzed. *Why is he taking it? Why doesn't he take the board from her?*

I lay crying in my bed, praying that the noise would stop. I imagined Mrs. Cummings flying from her house across the bay and standing guard at my window. The thought of her caring ways comforted my 8-year-old soul.

"Come forward, and receive Jesus." My dad spread his arms wide, inviting people to get right with God after his latest turn-to-God-or-roast-in-hell sermon.

The congregation sang a song with the same theme.

"Remember," Dad warned, "the only thing you can be sure of is the breath you just took."

Another song.

"If you have an accident on the way home, you'll get no more chances for heaven."

A third song.

"If you don't respond tonight, God might just quit knocking on the door of your heart."

Fear drove me forward. "Please, God," I sobbed, "don't send me to hell. Help me to be good so I can go to heaven."

whole

I trusted that Jesus would stand by my side as my own friend and keep me behaving. But, by Monday night, I'd do or think or feel something and know I was on the wrong side of God again.

We moved from California to Idaho during eighth grade. There we enjoyed the longest tenure of Dad's pastoring career — seven years. I managed to go to a single high school all four grades.

By my sophomore year of high school, I'd tired of my friendless, bottom-of-the-socially-accepted-ladder status. *I'll just shut up and observe the popular guys,* I vowed. *I want to be somebody.*

I watched and learned how to say the right things. I taught myself how to sound intelligent. I achieved my goal by my junior year, but felt empty, disillusioned.

An undercurrent of doom flowed beneath my success. Self-loathing caused me to view anyone who liked me with contempt.

How can you like a low-life like me? My self-motto became: *I hate who I was yesterday, but I will be different today.* So, if a classmate liked who I hated, I thought he was dumb and dropped him.

These conflicting thoughts brought on depression and serious thoughts of suicide. I needed to eliminate the person I hated — me.

The popular kids invited me to their parties. I went a few times, but getting drunk or stoned seemed dumb to me, and I quit going to parties. My social standing slipped, and I stood on the outside, looking in, again. Depression took hold. I flirted with suicide.

"Stop it," I said, blocking Mom's flailing fists. More than 6 feet tall, I towered over both parents, and I was tired of Mom's endless beatings on my sisters. I stepped between her and whichever kid was the subject of her immediate wrath and countered every blow. Mom tired of the bruising she'd get and let up on them.

Once, while fighting with both parents in the kitchen, I moved by Mom, holding a sandwich. She reached out and knocked it out of my hand, so I bent over to pick it up. She then hit the back of my head, so I grabbed her ankle and straightened up. She landed on her rear.

I left to work on my car in the garage. Dad joined me minutes later.

"If you were a gentleman," he said, "you'd apologize to your mother."

"I will," I answered, "when she acts like a lady."

I contracted pneumonia in November and couldn't go 30 seconds without a hacking cough. My parents ignored me, but after a week, Mom decided that maybe she should take me to a doctor.

He examined me and then turned to Mom. "We're going to admit him into the hospital," he said. "It's obvious he's not getting the care he needs at home." The sarcasm sailed right over her head.

Many days later, a young nurse announced, "The

doctor has discharged you." She smiled. "We're calling your parents now."

I dressed and then paced the room, happy to be getting out.

Fifteen minutes passed. Young Nurse returned, no longer smiling.

"I'm so sorry, John," she said, a frown puckering her forehead. "Your parents said they can't come today because they have to go to church tonight."

My shoulders slumped. *It's Wednesday,* I thought, berating myself. *What did you expect, Dumbo?*

The next morning, I noticed the floor seemed more still than normal.

"Why is it so quiet?" I asked another nurse. "Where is everybody?"

She peered at me. "It's Thanksgiving."

My parents managed to pick me up late in the day.

☙ ☙ ☙

"I surrender." Years of trying to please an unbending God ever ready (and maybe anxious) to toss me into hell and all my efforts at self-improvement versus self-loathing took its toll on my emotional state.

"I'm tired. Tired of trying to be someone I'm not. Tired of being depressed all the time."

I raised my hands in defeat. "You win, God. I lose. You'll always have the upper hand. Just please take away this depression."

shattered

My shoulders slumped. "I'll become a Christian, but I can't believe all the crap I've been raised with — a father, who is supposed to be a spiritual leader, beating the s*** out of me, and my siblings and my mother, the smiling, calm pastor's wife, screaming and hitting anyone in her way at home."

I sighed. "If you really want me to be a Christian, then you're going to have to show me what to believe."

It took years to seep in, but God began showing me things I could believe.

࿐࿐࿐

My friend Sam worked in a grocery store. I stopped by to see him at quitting time. We were messing around in the stockroom when he punched my arm and said, "Guess who likes you?"

"Huh?" I stared at him. Any female who found the me-who-hated-me attractive had to be unbalanced. "Who?"

"Barb." He punched my arm again.

"Who?" My mind went blank.

"Barb. My wife's sister. Your sister's roomie in college. That Barb." He snickered.

"She's three years older," I stated, shaking my head, searching for comprehension.

"And your point is?" Sam laughed again. "You tiger, you." Another friendly slap. "Go for it. Maybe you'll end up my brother-in-law."

He went home, leaving behind one badly confused

friend. My mind spun like cotton candy and felt just as dense.

Barb likes me? What does she possibly see in me?

Sam told his wife about our conversation. She called Barb.

"Guess who likes you?" she asked.

Soon after that, Barb's family invited me to go waterskiing with them.

The number one requirement on my list for a potential life mate was a normal family. Anything but how I'd been raised. Barb's family looked and acted normal to me — a point in her favor.

Late that summer, she helped me move into my dorm at the same college she attended, now in her senior year majoring in home economics.

Barb appeared stable, as did her family. I proceeded through dating with caution. *Marriage and children belong to folks who weren't wrapped too tight.* I didn't want to get entangled in the same web.

"People only marry for sex," I told Barb. "And kids are accidents from that."

"Give it a try," she urged. "Not everyone fights like your parents."

Even as we moved toward marriage, one thought remained with me. *I can always bail,* I thought as I waited by the altar for Barb to join me on our wedding day.

We married during Christmas break of my sophomore year. Barb's grandparents gave us a mobile home to live in, parked on their ranch. Six weeks later, I asked my dad to check out the wiring.

"You've got problems," he said. "I've fixed what I can for now, but you need a permanent solution."

We made an appointment to get insurance transferred in our names the next day, but the agent had left by the time we arrived.

"No problem," I said. "Tomorrow's Saturday. We'll come back first thing Monday."

On Sunday, I flipped on a light switch and saw smoke in the hallway.

"We've got to get this fixed, ASAP," I told Barb.

That night, the dog awakened me with his frantic barking. I saw flames and jumped out of bed. I shook Barb awake. "We have to get out of here," I shouted, "or we're toast!"

We dashed outside in our nightclothes. I grabbed my letterman jacket on our way out and tossed it on. My body heated up as I tried to fight the fire, and I tossed the jacket some 15 feet from the burning building. *Far enough,* I thought.

Everything in our home burned that night. Afterward, I went to retrieve the jacket. The fire had burned a path 12 inches wide, made a perfect right turn and attacked the coat.

Keep a light hold on any and all possessions, I mused.

Weeks later, Barb announced she was pregnant. Apprehension slammed into me. *What do I know of raising kids?* I thought.

whole

It evaporated the moment Barb laid our newborn daughter in my arms. *Hello, daughter.* I marveled at the perfect tiny life in my hands. *I'm a father.*

I touched her downy cheek. *Look at this incredible little person I've never met before, and yet, at this moment, I know I'd be willing to die for her.*

A son joined us three years later.

While not without conflict, marriage to Barb proved easier than I expected and never materialized into the nightmare I saw modeled by my parents. Even so, certain things Barb did reminded me of my mother. On those occasions, I'd punch her shoulder. I always felt terrible afterward and longed to overcome the urge.

જ∂જ∂જ∂

After the fire and with a baby coming, I knew going back to school was out of the question. I stepped into the bank next to the furniture company where I worked part-time and asked to see the manager.

"I'm looking for work," I said. "If any positions open up, will you please consider me?"

"Sure," he said. "Let's get started by filling out some paperwork."

The bank hired me as a teller and promoted me three years later as Operations Supervisor.

Sam worked as an EMT on an ambulance crew and talked me into joining him because they were short one man.

shattered

"I can't work the crew until I complete all the courses," I said.

"That's true," he agreed, "but we can make you designated driver until then."

"That sounds like a plan," I said.

A call came through at 1:30 a.m. the first night after I'd become a fully certified EMT. We raced to the scene, where a drunk had pulled out in front of a car.

We arrived, and my body switched to autopilot. The male victim showed signs of severe head trauma. I ran to the girl still in the car and pulled her out. I observed she was in complete cardiac arrest, so I began CPR, struggling to open her airway.

As I continued chest compressions, I glanced around the scene and noticed the crumpled car was a blue Toyota Celica.

That's interesting, I thought. *Cecilia has a blue Toyota Celica.*

Cecilia? One of the tellers I supervised at our small bank?

I glanced down at the girl under my palms and froze.

Cecilia. No, no! You can't die. You're only 19. Urgency surged through me. *Come on, Cecilia. Fight. You have to live. You have to!*

I wanted to bolt from the scene. Put it far from me. Make it never happen.

You have to stay.

I can't do this.

You must.

whole

"God," I cried out, "you have to help me. I can't do this."

Suddenly I felt a presence surrounding me. A presence more real to me than anyone or anything else at that scene.

The presence helped me do my job. I accompanied Cecilia to the hospital. The medical team got her heart going, but because she'd been oxygen deprived for a long period of time, her family decided not to keep her on life support. Her boyfriend died as well.

The knowledge of God's reality stayed with me.

Like my father, I began moving my family around from job to job. Unlike him, mine came in the form of promotions, not dissentions. But I remembered the emotional toll it took on me as a child to keep meeting new people and trying to fit in. I began turning down further promotions. Family would always come first for me.

In 1989, the opportunity came to purchase the same flower shop Barb had worked in during her college years. She wanted us to work together, like her parents did on their farm. I was less sure I'd enjoy the experience, but she pushed the idea, so I agreed.

What Barb remembered as a child, father and mother working side by side, failed to happen for us. She wanted to maintain full control of the store. I missed banking. My parents meddled in our marriage, seeking to drive a wedge between us.

shattered

One day, while I was kneeling down at home, I thought Barb hit the back of my head. As I rose, I grabbed her ankles and knocked her back onto the sofa.

"What's wrong with you?" she cried.

"You hit me." I shook my head to clear the memory of when my mom did the same.

"I did not," she said.

"Yes, you did."

She turned to our children. "Tell him," she said.

"She didn't touch you."

Depression and self-loathing returned. *I'd be better off to do myself in before I touch my children,* I decided. Only the fear of burning in hell kept me from actual suicide.

I decided to try counseling instead.

"Learn to use a punching bag," the counselor, Pat, suggested. "Or exercise until the frustration lifts."

Doesn't work, I thought. *I exercised like a fiend in high school. Never worked then. Won't work now.*

"This is a safe environment," Pat explained. "You can express whatever emotions you feel here."

Not a chance. Gotta hang tight to emotions. I've seen too much of how people abuse emotions.

I quit after four months and continued to stumble through life.

Barb and I decided to sell the flower shop two years later. I returned to banking, and she took on tutoring. Ten years passed.

❧❧❧

whole

"You have Post Traumatic Stress Disorder," Mary Ann, another counselor, told me.

"What?" I raked my fingers through my hair. "That's impossible. I'm not a vet."

"Possible," Mary Ann said. "You don't have to be a combat veteran to suffer PTSD. I've worked with many civilians suffering from PTSD. Mostly childhood trauma."

"Really?"

Maybe there is some hope for me.

With deliberate calm, Mary Ann began walking me through my life experiences.

"Do you realize you were spiritually abused?" Mary Ann asked in one of our sessions.

"*Spiritually abused?* What do you mean?"

"Think about it. Didn't your father use religion to control you?"

I thought about Dad's endless altar calls, warning if we didn't get right with God, we'd burn in hell forever.

"How did you handle that?"

"I tried so hard to stay on God's good side," I said.

"How did it go?"

"It was impossible. The more I tried, the more I failed. The more I failed, the more miserable I got, until I hated the very sight of me."

"Was there anybody in the church who could help?" Mary Ann asked.

"How?" I all but snorted. "My dad was the pastor. I was a PK — Preacher's Kid — and nothing less than perfection was expected of us. We put on our smiley faces at church, the image of the perfect, serene family, while at home, chaos reigned."

"You consider yourself a Christian?" she asked.

"Yes."

"Could you not turn to God as your heavenly father to help you?"

I stiffened. "I remember my professor in college saying something about, 'We view God as we view our father.'"

"You don't agree?"

"No, I remember thinking at that time, 'No way. God is righteous and fair. He's not petty or vindictive. He's not a liar.'"

"So, you don't equate your relationship with God as a father/son one?"

"No. I can't. Father spells bad, and I know that God is good."

"Do you believe that?" Mary Ann asked.

"Yes, I do," I said. "The Old Testament declares God's goodness over and over again." I spread my fingers. "He's good. I'm the bad one."

"How do you rate yourself as a Christian?" she asked.

"Third-, maybe even fourth-rate."

"Why?"

"Because I keep on messing up," I said.

We worked together for several months. One day Mary Ann asked, "Were you ever sexually abused?"

"No!"

But as the therapy progressed, a memory, like a single bubble in a pond, rose. I saw Mom naked. Nudity in any form was strictly forbidden in our home. *I'm just stressed out,* I thought. *No way had I ever seen Mom naked. No way.*

I popped the bubble. It returned again and again.

That single bubble continued to surface with increasing regularity. Then a second joined it. Mom touching me. I trembled. *What demon has taken over my mind? No way these things happened.*

A year after my first session with Mary Ann, Barb and I went camping. As I sat alone, immersed in the beauty of God's creation, I saw dozens of bubbles rising in the pond of my memory.

"Oh, my gosh. Oh, my gosh." I panted for breath. "It happened. It really happened." My thoughts rushed back to when I was 5, the only child at home during the day, because my sisters were at school.

Mom really did expose herself to me, repeatedly, and … and … My breath came in bunches. *She fondled me.* Sorrow overwhelmed me.

Jesus stated that "the truth will set you free." As I shared my memories with Mary Ann, healing began.

కొకొకొ

Barb and I both contracted the flu right after Christmas. I started to improve, but she couldn't seem to shake it. She'd been slowing down due to fibromyalgia and had to cut down on tutoring.

I took her to the emergency room. The doctor

examined her and sent her back home with a prescription. I dropped her off at home, then drove around looking for a pharmacy that was open after hours.

The next morning, I tried to awaken her.

"Unnnn …"

"You feeling any better?" I asked.

"I feel I could die from this," she said, stumbling to get herself dressed. "Call the ambulance."

"I can't breathe," Barb said, after we'd arrived at the Emergency Room. The doctors ran more tests and then called me into a private room.

"We're seeing some anomalies," one said. "We'd like to run more tests, but we aren't equipped to do it here."

"Where should we go?" I asked.

"You can go to Ontario," the doctor said, "it being closer. However, it's New Year's Eve, and there won't be anyone there to read the tests."

"What's my second option?" I asked.

"We can airlift her to Boise, which is what I would recommend," he said. "We can get the tests run and read quicker."

"Let's do it," I said. I went home to pack for the 70-mile trip and called my children.

When I returned, Barb had a breathing tube down her throat. Her pulse dropped to 17, and the doctor began CPR.

"Don't worry, John," he said, "we just need to jumpstart her."

whole

I'm an EMT. I've seen too many scenes just like this. I sat down and dropped my head in my hands. *Oh, gosh, this is it.*

Barb died there by the helicopter, 4 p.m., New Year's Eve.

I returned home some 12 hours later, exhausted and still in shock. I fell into bed and squeezed my eyes shut.

"I'm sorry, I'm so sorry, Barb," I sobbed. Suddenly, it was as if I saw her standing by the bed, through my closed lids. She stood fresh, young, vibrant, Barb as she was when we first married.

It's all right, John, I felt her say. *I know you love me.*

While I wrestled with guilt, not being able to save my wife, the doctors suggested an autopsy because nobody could explain her death. It revealed Barb had an enlarged heart. Nobody knew of it. The drugs plus the Nyquil she'd taken to sleep had strained her already weakened heart.

"It's not your fault." I heard the words, but my heart and brain had a hard time processing them.

A year later, loneliness threatened to shut me down emotionally. I remembered a mutual friend, Connie, whom Barb and I'd known since high school.

I called her.

"Hi, Connie," I said. "Please don't take this the wrong way, but do you think we could go places together? I just need to get out."

"Sure." Connie laughed. "I'm game."

We began doing things together as friends.

shattered

"Want to come to church with me?" Connie asked.

"Where?" I asked.

"Christian Life Fellowship," she said. "In Ontario."

"Sure, I'll go."

I walked in the door, emotional armor in place and buckled, prepared to face another group of fake Christians.

"Nobody plays at being a Christian there," I said as we drove away after the service. "Everyone seemed genuine."

"Of course," Connie said. "I've been going to this church for 30 years. These folks are as real as it gets."

"Never much cared for the label 'Christian,'" I said. "Saw too many hypocrites growing up. I felt I never measured up."

"Measured up to what?" Connie asked.

"Man's standards. God's standards," I replied. "No matter how much I read the Bible or prayed or tried to do the right thing, I always felt inadequate, like a third- or fourth-rate Christian."

"That's a lie, straight from the devil," Connie said. "We are all number one with God."

I continued attending CLF with Connie. Week after week, I sat under Biblical teaching, inching my way to the realization that God views me as first-rate, because I'm his son, and he loves me.

Connie and I discovered we shared many interests. Enough to join ourselves in marriage in June of 2009. As I grow in our marriage, I am also growing in God.

I observe the people of CLF much as I once watched

my classmates. They model healthy emotion and worship with abandon.

I realize I'm not doomed to live as I was raised. I know someday my emotions will heal, so I can express them from my heart and not just my head. Meanwhile, I allow God to draw me closer and closer, trusting him, my genuine and proper father.

conclusion

Nobody is perfect. We all have a past. But it is what we do with our future that matters. We all have messes in our lives, mistakes we've made.

By embracing God's transformational power and love, we all can trust him to restore, rebuild and renew our lives.

I strongly believe that within these stories, God's love is shining through.

If you believe in your heart that God has a future of healing and wholeness for you, you are welcome to join a group of Christ-followers every Sunday morning at Christian Life Fellowship (CLF), located only three blocks south of Taco Bell. Our members aren't perfect, but are filled with open hearts, open minds and tons of love for you.

If you're not able to join us at the church building, we offer support online at our Web site: www.clfontario.org. From there, you can e-mail in prayer requests, listen to Bible teachings online and see what we have to offer you and your family (when you do feel comfortable joining us).

You don't have to be a Bible scholar to start your relationship with God. God is always surrounding you. He cares greatly for you, your family and friends. So speak with him directly.

shattered

You could start with the ABCs of faith:

A stands for admitting. The Bible reads, "For all have sinned and fall short of the glory (or standard) of God" (Romans 3:23). Each one of us, as Christians, have admitted that we have disobeyed and fallen short.

B stands for believing in Jesus Christ. "For God loved the world so much that he gave his one and only Son, so that everyone who believes in him will not perish but have eternal life" (John 3:16). Jesus was sent from heaven to erase all the sins of mankind, and God raised him from the dead. If you believe in him and seek after him, you will have life and have it abundantly.

C stands for confessing. "If you confess with your mouth that Jesus is Lord and believe in your heart that God raised him from the dead, you will be saved. For it is by believing in your heart that you are made right with God, and it is by confessing with your mouth that you are saved" (Romans 10:9-10). Believing in our hearts and confessing with our mouths brings us to salvation. Being saved means we are now forgiven of all sins. It means we are now ready to love God, be free of the past and live forever in God's favor while on earth and eventually in heaven for eternity.

If you are ready and want to start a relationship with God and begin your amazing adventure as a Christian, pray this suggested prayer or make it your own:

conclusion

Lord Jesus, I know I am separated from you, but I want to change that. I am sorry for the choices I've made that have broken your laws. I believe your death paid for my sins, and you are now alive to change me from the inside out. Would you please do that now? God, I receive your love and forgiveness right now. Thank you for hearing and changing me. Now please help me know you in a relational way, so I can experience life as it was meant to be. In Jesus' name I pray. Amen.

If you meant that prayer, you are now experiencing the love and forgiveness of God. His power is being released in you, and real life is beginning! Don't let it end there — share your story of reaching out to God with someone, and reach out to us at CLF, where someone will offer to talk and pray with you more about this journey of faith. God loves you, and so do we!

Pastor Doug Hezeltine
Christian Life Fellowship
Ontario, Oregon
www.clfontario.org

We would love for you to join us at Christian Life Fellowship!

We meet Sunday mornings at 9 and 11 a.m. at 366 SE 5th Street, Ontario, OR 97914.

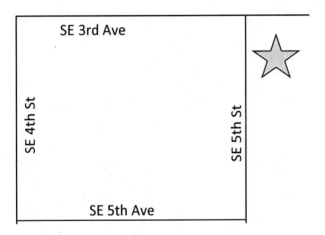

Please call us at 541.889.7264 for directions, or contact us at www.clfontario.org.

For more information on reaching your city with
stories from your church, go to
www.testimonybooks.com.

GOOD CATCH
PUBLISHING

Did one of these stories touch you?
Did one of these real people move you to tears?
Tell us (and them) about it on our Facebook page at
www.facebook.com/GoodCatchPublishing.